St. Louis Community College

Library

5801 Wilson Avenue
St. Louis, Missouri 63110

HELP FOR YOUR GRIEF

HELP
FOR YOUR
GRIEF

Dr. Arthur Freese

SCHOCKEN BOOKS · NEW YORK

First published by SCHOCKEN BOOKS 1977

Copyright © 1977 by Arthur S. Freese

Library of Congress Cataloging in Publication Data

Freese, Arthur S
Help for your grief.

Bibliography: p. 197
Includes index.
1. Grief. I. Title.

BF575.G7F73   155.9′37   76-44538

Manufactured in the United States of America

TO MY BROTHER, SIG:

although he died during my work on this book, he
will always live within me and in my writing. . . .

One generation passeth away, and another generation cometh:
but the earth abideth forever.

Ecclesiastes 1:4

Contents

III: THE SPECIFIC HELP FOR YOUR GRIEF

Acknowledgments

Still within me too are memories of Elliott Gray Young (whose death three years ago first sparked the idea for this book) and his daughter Alison, Stanley Lewis, and last but not least my friend and teacher Professor Beatrice Schapper.

And there are those whose help made this book possible: Dr. Vamik D. Volkan, whose vast knowledge of grief and mourning combined with a warm human understanding to illuminate so much in this field that it is impossible to pay tribute to him adequately; Dr. Joseph L. Bell, whose wisdom and insights helped immeasurably in making it possible for me to understand and see the real meaning of death and of life—and their intimate connection; Dr. Pietro Castelnuovo-Tedesco, whose rich knowledge of psychiatry has been put at my disposal so often; Dr. Theodore B. Cohen, who was so generous with his time; Dr. George H. Pollock and too many others to be mentioned in so short a space. Thanks are particularly due to the American Psychoanalytic Association and the rich resourses of its membership.

My appreciation also goes out to my editor, Seymour Barofsky, who gave so freely of himself and his time—and who fortunately had so much personally to give. And my thanks to my wife Ruth who had to suffer through the writing of this book at a time when I myself was struggling with the very grief work described here.

HELP FOR YOUR GRIEF

Introduction: The Promise of Help—Gain for Your Loss

Sincere serious books about sex are not pornographic—nor is this book on grief sorrowful. Rather, it is a book of hope and of promise. For to talk about grief is to talk about life, to talk of loss is also to talk of gain. A psychiatrist who has worked a great deal with children and adolescents told me that the first signs of hope and health in his young patients were when they began to talk of death—for there is no concern or interest in death until one wants to live. So to talk about grief is also to talk about life and growth—and there can be no growth without grief.

While bereavement and grief are the most universal of all human experiences—and the most human—they are also the most painful. And this book, simply, is about the twin problems of growth and grief. It is intended to provide the very information needed for one to lose one's fear of grief and to show how to grow with grief, how to find gain in the much more obvious loss.

The distinction between the terms bereavement and grief are commonly slight and the two are often used interchangeably. To distinguish between the two, grief is the specific human reaction to a loss, while bereavement is the total process that goes on as a result of grief—that bereavement includes grief along with all the

1

processes of healing and recovery from the grief or loss, even the mourning which may be formal (wearing black, for example) and outside, as well as the grief that is inside.

None of us can escape bereavement, the loss of loved ones. But we can make this agonizing period less painful, less frightening and certainly far less destructive than it is to most people. This can only be done, however, by knowing what others go through so that we are not caught unprepared and unawares, are not overwhelmed but know the best ways to gain help, to help ourselves, even to help others. I myself am just coming through this experience—and knowledge *does* help. There are often strange, bizarre, but rarely spoken of sensations, thoughts, changes, that toss us about in the power and caprice of the resulting emotional tornado. Help comes from recognizing those normal human reactions that all of us undergo in highly individual degrees and widely varying combinations and forms during this most shaking and deepest of all human experiences.

The overwhelming effect of the death of a loved person lies in the very nature of the phenomenon of separation—probably the most basic and painful of all human experiences. Yet this is a situation every one of us must suffer through again and again during our lifetimes, for it all starts with the trauma of birth. In the separation from the mother, the infant is forced out from the warmth and protected stability of the womb. Totally provided for in the uterus and sheltered from all change, the newborn infant is suddenly thrust forth into a world of harsh noises and glaring lights, of changing temperatures and sudden breezes, an existence in which this tiny, immature new creature must for the first time carry out all its own functions. Its initial wail is really a cry of protest against the pain of separation—and the innumerable separations this new human being will repeatedly undergo will each time stir up reminders of this first traumatic incident of its life.

There are the pain and trauma of growth with its necessary separations during childhood. Early in life the infant must give up the breast and later it toddles away from Mother to explore the world in its home, only to be frightened by straying too far from Mother, by separating. Fright turns to terror when the separation hints at permanent loss, when the mother can no longer be located, as in a crowd. School involves another separation, and the storminess of the teens arises in large part from the tearing separations that are experienced as the adolescent grows away from the parents and matures into the man or woman.

In those instances where parents prevent this separation, there is no growth and the adult remains tied to the mother's apron strings (often very subtly and perhaps only emotionally). This failure to mature may occur because the separation is too painful or because the parents have fought it instead of encouraging, easing and teaching the child to grow. Thus growth and change occur only through separation (from past or parents or whatever) which in turn offers opportunities for growth and change (maturation and mutation, if you will)—in short, this is truly a two-way street.

Life brings with it one separation after another, each with its load of pain. There are the separations when the young adult leaves home for schooling in a distant community, and those when adulthood leads young people on to careers in distant places. Simply moving from one home to another is a tearing apart, too, and Americans change their residences with almost incredible frequency today. It's common to leave one job for another and, ultimately, there is the disassociation of retirement: statistics probe the traumatic nature of separation and loss in the increased health problems and rising mortality following life's separations (say, retirement or divorce or the loss of one's job).

But stretching virtually through all ages there is the shadow of death, the ultimate and permanent separation. Death is feared because for the dying person it is the total dissociation from everything held dear and worthwhile—the forfeiture of seeing the sun and feeling the rain, of the beauties of the day and the night and the many things in the world about us, the end of being with loved ones and career and of all future. For the bereaved, the survivors, there is also a permanent but certainly less total separation, one in which they lose for all time a particular person. Thomas Mann in *The Magic Mountain* looked at all this from a personal perspective: "A man's dying is more the survivor's affair than his own." So there need be little surprise that bereavement has vast affects (emotions and feelings and affects are terms often used interchangeably, meaning virtually the same)—bizarre and deep-seated psychic reactions with long-lasting components.

Edgar Allan Poe suffered more than most, for that poet lost both parents when he was only three. His adored wife ("the lost Lenore") died after an eleven-year marriage and his grief resulted in a poem, "The Raven," which established his fame. In this poem, the bizarre bird comes to perch above the poet's chamber door in "the bleak December" (holiday seasons are always difficult for the bereaved) when he was himself seeking ". . . surcease of sorrow . . . for the lost Lenore—"

As all great artists, Poe had an intuitive insight into the human psyche, an understanding which was first explained scientifically by Sigmund Freud. The poet wove his fancies about this bird which could speak but a single word—"Nevermore." He saw the raven as having been sent him by his God to provide:

"Respite—respite and nepenthe from thy memories of Lenore;
Quaff, oh, quaff this kind nepenthe and forget this lost Lenore!"
            Quoth the Raven, "Nevermore."

As the poem builds to its climax, Poe ends with:

"Take thy beak from out my heart, and take thy form from off my
    door!"
            Quoth the Raven, "Nevermore."

And the Raven, never flitting, still is sitting—*still* is sitting. . . .
And the lamp-light o'er him streaming throws his shadow on the
    floor;

And my soul from out that shadow that lies floating on the floor
Shall be lifted—nevermore!

Thus are the basic truths of mankind captured in the imagery of great creative artists. Mann was calling attention to the anguish of the bereaved, while Poe recognized the permanence of loss and grief, how the dead person lives on within the survivors. In fact, Poe's sense of almost total despair in "The Raven" is one that is common during the initial stages of grief, as we shall see later.

But with knowledge one can learn to do the necessary grief work, to carry out the task of mourning so that bereavement finally becomes not a burden but a positive thing to help one grow in freedom. As in all great artistic and religious works, the patterns of grief and mourning are recognized in the Bible too, as we shall see from the quotations with which we begin our chapters. In it, too, there is an awareness that only through grief and mourning can there be recovery from the loss. The person who shirks this mourning task, who represses or denies his or her grief (who "doesn't give in") will never come out from that shadow on the floor, will never be free of the tyranny of the past.

Grief work in many ways is not unlike childbirth—both are painful, but both, when carried through successfully, can bring forth something worthwhile. There is no magical way to escape the suffering of grief any more than there is one to escape the pain that follows surgery or severe disease: we must endure in order to recover. Grief, too, is an illness, a wound that heals slowly, often erratically, and always painfully. But let us now look briefly at some of the forms that grief can take.

It has long been said that those who lose a loved one may die of a "broken heart." Today's America puts such proverbs and folk sayings in a class with sassafras tea and asafetida as the relics of a superstitious past, forgetting that adages are often a matter of deep folk wisdom finely honed by tens of thousands of years of accurate observation and verbal polishing. Only recently a scientific study of widowers revealed that these men who have lost loved ones do indeed die of "broken hearts"—for the chief cause of death among these bereaved are heart attacks and heart disease, and the closely related hardening of the arteries.

This physical toll of grief is far more readily understandable than the strange nightmarish affects which cause sufferers the most trouble—unless these are expected and so not feared. Half or more of mourners, for example, have hallucinations—see or hear or feel the deceased person. Such hallucinations are in fact a normal and healthy concomitant of the grieving process in almost all instances. Unfortunately, mourners are reluctant and ashamed to talk of this and so never learn how many have these same experiences. One middle-aged woman recently revealed to me how she had been told some forty years ago that a widow had heard her dead husband speaking. My informant had never mentioned this before and did so to me only because I was the first to spell out specifically to her how often this sort of thing actually happened and how common and normal it was—in the United States and in London, in Wales and Japan, and probably everywhere else as well.

During the initial grief period there may be an inability to remember the deceased person, to the point where the survivor can't even recall what the dead person looked like. There may be numbness and an inability to do anything—or a terrible restlessness making it impossible for the sufferer to sit in one spot too long, to attend a meeting or see a movie, to worship in a church. Some develop tremors or begin to stammer, while others may even suffer broken bones as a result of losing their sense of balance and falling continually (I twisted my ankle three times in a single day, something I never did before). One man I know kept losing track of his train of thought in the middle of his sentences, another could no longer remember the phone numbers of friends.

A woman found it impossible to make change and another couldn't find her way home from work even though she had been going this same way for years. A very gentle widow became a spitting, abusive virago, exploding violently on the mildest provocation, or even on none at all. Feelings and moods shift frequently and unaccountably—some bereaved persons can't sleep at all, while others do so all the time, and the same person may go through both phases at different times. There may be a wild craving for sex—or no desire at all: the patterns change often and can create the greatest guilt and anxiety for those who don't recognize that this is just another of the common experiences among those who go through grieving.

To comprehend this strange process, it's necessary to learn something of psychiatric concepts and viewpoints. Actually we do this all the time—we say, "I have rocks in my stomach," and strangely this emotional expression feels just that way physically. Human beings also use symbols to express or hide their real emotions: one man once told me how when he met people he would first look at their fingernails and then their teeth. Here was a clear expression of anger, of hostility, for "tooth and nail" is the classic and primitive method of attacking another person or animal.

And so it goes—one person won't be able to control his eating, while another can't touch food, or both may go through different periods of each set of reactions. These waves of responses and emotions roll over the sufferers like ground fogs, rising and falling, appearing and disappearing, behaving unpredictably and erratically. As for the eating—the mourner is so filled with grief that there is no room left for food, or so empty from the loss that there is a desperate craving for food even though no quantity is capable of filling the enormous emotional void left by the death of a loved one.

Nor does grief wear off in any simple manner, say like a cold. The return to the former normality is a slow, complex, episodic process with many ups and downs. The grieving person can never be really sure just how he or she will be at any particular time or place. I attended a Christmas party with some anticipation, hoping to enjoy many old friends, only to become so depressed that I was glad to escape and it took two days to snap back. But the rocky road does—with knowledge and with help if necessary—smooth out eventually. (I enjoy parties again, now.)

All in all, grief is a strange, otherworldly sort of period whose length is totally unpredictable except in broad outline, in years, and not days or weeks or even months. We'll study some guidelines later in our book which will point up the differences between the healthy "good grief" and the pathological or prolonged mourning. Yet out of all this, given knowledge and understanding, the mourner can grow and mature, find himself or herself a richer and happier person after the mourning has been finally and fully worked through, and end up with a better and more satisfying life than ever before.

Repeatedly I've heard mourners complain: "Why didn't someone tell me it was going to be like this?" And this is what our book is all about—to answer this question, to offer guidelines and some advice and information. In short, to help the bereaved to know "good grief" and learn to use it. So let us now move on to the details and the help we have promised here.

PART I
THE BASICS FOR GROWTH WITH GRIEF

CHAPTER ONE

The Natural History of Grief: What the Bereaved Can Expect

To every thing there is a season, and a time
to every purpose under the heaven:
A time to be born, and a time to die;

Ecclesiastes 3:1-2

It was Boston on Saturday, November 28, 1942, the day of the big
Boston College-Holy Cross football game. That evening some
eight hundred celebrants, mostly young and many in service
uniforms, crowded into Boston's oldest nightclub, the Cocoanut
Grove, to dance, drink and dine. About ten o'clock a young
busboy struck a match to replace a light bulb and changed our
world when his match touched an imitation palm tree. When a few
minutes later the dance band struck up ''The Star-Spangled Ban-
ner'' to herald the floor show, a girl suddenly burst across the
dance floor with her hair ablaze and her voice screaming ''Fire!''

The guests panicked wildly, but in trying to escape, they only
succeeded in jamming the revolving-door exits. Flames quickly
raced through the club—blazing draperies fell on terror-stricken
guests, women had gowns and hair set afire, some people were
knocked down and flung under tables while others were actually
trampled to death. Many stumbled on the six-foot-wide stairway
leading to the exits, and others tried to scramble over the fallen
until soon there were actually layers of dead bodies.

The night was filled with the wail of sirens as fire engines and
ambulances from nearby navy installations joined Boston's own

emergency equipment. The fire was quickly brought under control, but not until it had taken its toll. For six hours the charred bodies were brought out from the ruins. Doctors and nurses provided what first aid they could while Catholic priests administered last rites. The streets about the club were littered with bodies, a neighboring garage and store were converted to emergency use and became temporary morgues. Every possible vehicle—trucks, taxis, private cars, vans, whatever—was pressed into service to transport the dead, the dying and the injured alike to hospitals whose lobbies were soon filled with bodies.

When it was all over, 492 people had died and some 200 were hospitalized—barely a hundred escaped unhurt. The cataclysmic disaster left hundreds, perhaps thousands, of families bereft of children, brothers and sisters, parents, nieces and nephews, the whole gamut of relatives, along with friends and co-workers, and the many other meaningful relationships of a complex modern society. Yet ultimately even this tragedy—like grief itself—produced growth and change. For this terrible fire led to an understanding of bereavement that has made possible both help and hope for all of mankind. From this tragedy the medical experts have learned how to deal with grief—and in a sense even this book has grown out of that Cocoanut Grove catastrophe.

At Boston's great Massachusetts General Hospital during the time of that city's nightclub calamity, there was a young psychiatrist, Dr. Erich Lindemann. This physician studied the reactions of the fire's survivors and those of the families of the victims, and out of this welter of misery a distinct pattern emerged. Lindemann's classic report spelled a recognition of the dimensions and problems of grief, and experts still regard his article as the definitive and basic one on this subject ("Symptomatology and Management of Acute Grief," published in the *American Journal of Psychiatry* in 1944).

Before we examine Lindemann's findings, however, let us first see how mankind's attitudes and feelings about death as well as its fears have altered until they've come to those we see about us today.

The Fear of Death

Man's attitude toward death has changed considerably just as man himself has in the nearly five million years he is currently believed to have been around. Yet through this long development it's really only been the last half century or so that man has ceased to walk hand in hand with death, has lost his view of death as a natural, normal and comfortable companion. I can recall how my ninety-two-year-old grandmother died in my home. She lived with my parents and myself about 1933, and there was even then no thought of sending her to the hospital although her death was known to be a matter of a few weeks away at the most. But dying at home is almost unheard of today when the hospital has suddenly become the place where we now bring our days to a close in a cold, sterile, unfriendly atmosphere peopled by uninvolved strangers.

One reason for this alteration in our feelings about death lies in the fact that death is no longer as close at hand as it once was. After all, Neanderthal man had an average life span of only some twenty-six years, while the ancient Greeks and Romans could look to perhaps an average of a mere twenty-seven years. Medieval Englishmen didn't do much better—barely over thirty years— while Americans at the turn of our own century lived on the average less than fifty years. Until the post-World War II medical era, there were really no ways in which physicians could stop the many diseases (such as pneumonia) which usually caused death then, for we had no antibiotics, no steroids, and so on. Even aspirin was discovered only at the turn of the century.

Man's former acceptance and intimacy with death was exemplified in that old nursery rhyme in which the child queries his physician who then replies:

"Doctor, Doctor, will I die?
Yes, my child, and so shall I."

Both are familiar and comfortable with death and accept its inevitability. Yet despite this easy familiarity with death, man has always feared his own personal end and it shows in his mythology going back into the farthest reaches of distant time.

For the hero—that rare one, different and set apart from and above the rest of us—has always been the one for whom death holds no terrors. This is true even today when the brave man is still the person who either deliberately sacrifices his life for another or at least puts his life in jeopardy, not in ignorance or without fear but in the full acceptance of that underlying terror of death we all share. Interestingly, however, the great folk heroes are the ones who conquer death—unlike the rest of us, to these heroes death does not come, but like Charlemagne and King Arthur they only sleep, to arise again when they are needed or in the hour of their destiny.

Dr. Pietro Castelnuovo-Tedesco, Vanderbilt University professor of psychiatry and one of America's leading psychoanalysts, explains the fear of death that we all feel because it is "the final and ultimate death of the organism, the full obliteration of the self." And this brings us back to the issue we raised in the Introduction. As Dr. Tedesco puts it: "Losses of other people also remind us of our own mortality and our own vulnerability—essentially the issue of loss." The awareness of this relationship between death, separation and loss is well put in the French adage: "To say good-bye is to die a little."

With the changing attitudes toward death, the question of whether this fear is only a recent matter naturally arises. But as Dr. Tedesco sees it: "There's no reason to believe that people felt any differently in the past than they do now. . . . I'm sure the problems were the same, only some of the solutions were different."

Solving Death's Terror: That Old-Time Religion

Religion is one of the different solutions of the past. Increasingly, today's Americans are likely to laugh at those who seriously believe in an actual afterlife, a life after death in which there is a conscious and usually a physical existence. A public opinion poll in 1961 found that three-quarters of all Americans believe in an afterlife, but Dr. Glenn M. Vernon, University of Utah professor of sociology, in a study of his own found the percentage of those believing in an afterlife much lower among college-age people—only a quarter, for example, of those with no religious affiliations.

However, I found that these beliefs have now come full circle and are on the rise again—only now they are showing themselves among those who follow the occult rather than the reduced numbers following the conventional religions. I found these beliefs in mysticism definitely on the rise even among the new young physicians, many of whom are delving into the realms of the occult and following doctrines which would have been laughed out of any medical or scientific gathering as recently as a decade or so ago.

Those who sincerely believe in a real afterlife gain a great deal from their belief, where it is limited to that world after death which we cannot know—what is variously called "heaven" or "another dimension" or whatever. Psychiatrists today consistently recognize the traditional religious belief in a life after death and one's own personal immortality as a supportive and useful creed. Dr. Tedesco points out the difficulties of truly believing there is *no* afterlife: "To accept this idea of passing into nothingness is very disturbing to our sense of narcissism." But for those who *do* believe in an afterlife: "Death for these people doesn't mean total annihilation but simply passing on to another world where one would hope to meet one's friends, relatives, and other people whose company one had enjoyed."

One thing however that is clear from man's history is . . .

The Changing Attitudes Toward Death

As our early legends revealed—the knights of the Round Table and the paladins of Charlemagne—the dying person of those days recognized his or her own approaching death and prepared for it by lying down in the accepted fashion, composing himself and thinking the appropriate thoughts, even making the socially correct remarks and so on. In short, it was a highly ritualized death and spoken of readily and openly—and the very security of knowing what to do and what was to come (the life after death as their religion promised) was both very helpful and immensely comforting.

This pattern which Phillipe Aries, the pioneer French social historian, calls "Tamed Death" was the order of the day until the nineteenth century. Its familiarity and simplicity caused people neither to shrink from it nor hide from its mention or its sight. Passersby in the streets would join the priest on his way to administer the last rites, and together all would attend the dying even though strangers. Besides the relatives, friends and other adults, children, too, were always part of any deathbed scene.

From this very natural setup, Aries points out, death became— starting in the nineteenth century—wild, forbidden and shameful. But now there would seem at least an attempt to make this all come full cycle again as there is an attempt at an increased and open talk of death. The 1974 Pulitzer Prize for general nonfiction went to Ernest Becker's best seller, *The Denial of Death*, yet this book recognized the overwhelming fear of death under whose shadow we pass our days and then went on to call for a turning to a modern version of that old-time religion. Becker looked toward a new cooperation between science and religion and even perhaps heroism to resolve man's haunting and lifelong fear and denial of death.

Our current attitudes toward this problem have even been described as

"The Pornography of Death"

Increasingly the investigators of the modern attitude toward death are seeing it as taking the form described by Dr. Geoffrey Gorer, highly respected English anthropologist, who speaks of "the pornography of death," a situation in which death is now treated with that same avoidance and prudery that the Victorians and those even up to a generation or so ago treated sex. In short, death has become an "unmentionable"—just as sex was as recently as the first part of our own century. Yet in the memory of many living Americans, people died in their own homes and the bodies were prepared for burial by families and friends.

But somehow prudery shifted from sex to death, and now death is a "don't talk about it in front of the children" bit. Obviously just as sex dominates the first part of our lives, so death does in the second part—and Ernest Becker feels the fear of death is the powerful driving force throughout our lives. In any case we were certainly unsuccessful in repressing sex—and we will surely be if the same tactic is applied now to death.

To understand and come to grips with grief, we have to do so with death, and Americans are increasingly unprepared to cope with the problem. To understand death and grief we must realize we are a little like the blindmen and the elephant where each man described a different aspect he touched (tail or trunk or leg or whatever). Like blindmen we too can only appreciate one aspect at a time and we have already looked at several. Let us now turn to another aspect of death, one which intimately involves grief and the problems of the bereaved.

The American Pattern of Death and Grief—and Their Taboos

To understand our seemingly strange ways of dealing with death and grief today, we must also comprehend the nature of "taboo." The very word comes from the Polynesian *tabu* and in general means "forbidden." It first came into use some two hundred years ago during discussions of religion. Taboo became the equivalent of sacred, but "taboo" was an ambivalent, a two-sided concept involving both the holy and the dangerous, the pure and the impure, the protective and the prohibited. The sacred was on the one hand a power carrying blessings and holiness while—on the other—it brought death and pollution.

Where talk of sex was taboo to the Victorians and those early in our own century, death has now assumed this role—at a time when, almost simultaneously, the taboo nature of sex is subsiding. Dr. Glenn Vernon points out that the high taboo nature of death is revealed by the very way our movies keep the viewers from identifying with those characters slated for death. And in murder movies, instead of the normal grief for the victim, there is the pursuit of the murderer. But nowhere is grief truly portrayed in all its difficulty and confusion. However, by handling murder movies in this manner, contact with grief is avoided while death leads to action instead of bereavement.

Vernon also probes the strange nature of our national attitude toward death as shown, for example, in a study by Dr. Robert Fulton, University of Minnesota professor of sociology: those who refused to complete a questionnaire on this topic proved to be chiefly among those who live on the East and West coasts. Nearly half (40 percent) of those who did respond reported they rarely or never thought about death or dying, while 12 to 14 percent thought about it frequently or all the time. Obviously, there must be something taboo about death to cause so many people to ignore a part of life that touches every one of us every single day. For, after all, it is literally impossible to peruse a newspaper without reading about someone's death, either in the headlines or on the obituary page, in the reports of murders and crimes and other fatal violence, of auto and plane accidents.

Since death is taboo, a stigma is attached to it and, as a result, people avoid funerals and even shun talking about death itself. The bereaved, too, are evaded, for the mourner now bears some of this stigma (the mark of Cain if you will)—his or her conversations are turned away from the death or the deceased even though the sufferer wants and needs to talk about this, as we shall see later. The mourner becomes—as I have experienced recently—a sort of "untouchable" who is avoided or dealt with in an embarrassed and awkward fashion. In short, the mourner finds himself or herself held at arm's length. It's as if the mourner too has become tainted with death, is now a carrier of this contagion.

This taboo spreads to include everything touching death. Take, for example, a fifty-year-old writer I know who won't read the obituary page in his local newspaper. There are many like this writer who won't take out life insurance to protect their families, or won't draw up wills, for these actions, too, touch on death and have become taboo. The only ones who freely approach and deal with mourners are those who themselves have suffered a bereavement, who themselves carry this contagion of death and so cannot be affected.

But the understanding of grief goes back—as does the overwhelming bulk of psychiatry and psychology—to . . .

The Genius of Sigmund Freud

The appreciation of Freud's towering genius increases with each additional area that modern psychiatry probes in depth, and grief and mourning are no exception. Some sixty years ago, Freud wrote two papers on "Mourning and Melancholia" (this last term is no longer commonly used but is what we today term "depression").

Freud pointed out in these articles that grief is a reaction to the loss of a loved one, that it is *not* a pathological (disease) condition but a normal one, that it was *not* to be treated medically (as we shall see in our chapter on pills and grief). Freud noted the painfulness of mourning, the loss of interest by the bereaved in the world outside, the inability to love, the restriction or inhibition of all activity, the guilt feelings. He even recognized the regression that occurs in the bereaved. Nothing was added to Freud's discussion for a generation (some twenty-seven years to be exact) until Erich Lindemann wrote his classic report on the survivors and relatives in that Cocoanut Grove fire.

The Pattern of Acute Grief

In his study of the aftermath of the Cocoanut Grove catastrophe, Erich Lindemann uncovered what happens to people in acute grief and concluded that there were five groups of reactions in this situation. We will merely outline these in general terms here, for many of them will have entire chapters devoted to them later in our book:

First, there are the physical sensations—these are the sort of things you yourself have experienced and accepted as a part of fear. There may be a tightening of the throat or a shortness of breath, a sighing that comes on almost of its own volition. There may also be an emptiness inside the sufferer, a hunger, some muscular weakness and so on.

Then there is often an intense preoccupation with thoughts of the dead person.

Hostility and anger appear—and usually marked guilt feelings.

And, finally, there are the disturbances of the normal behavior patterns of the individual.

This whole process may go on for a matter of months, a year or more. How successfully the process is carried out depends on the "grief work," the mourning process, which involves three elements: the freeing of the mourner from the bondage to the one who has died; a readjustment to a new life situation without the deceased; and, lastly, the building of new relationships.

The success of this grief work is dependent also on how well the mourner overcomes the very human tendency to avoid the pain and distress of grief and the desire to evade the expression of the sufferer's true emotions. Lindemann was aware, too, of the danger these bereaved run of being stricken by physical illnesses should they fail to carry out the grief work, should they be unable to express the emotions of grief. But it was twenty years after Lindemann's study that confirmation of his findings came from another unexpected and very tragic occurrence.

Grief for a Nation: President Kennedy's Assassination

John F. Kennedy's assassination produced an enormous outpouring of intense personal feelings on a national basis for a variety of reasons. Our president, as the nation's top executive and leader, is naturally an authority figure, a parental figure (speaking symbolically of course). But, in addition, John Kennedy's age at the time (he was only forty-six) caused older people to react to him as to a son, teenagers as to a father, and to the middle-aged the suddenness of the death stirred up all the fears of a heart attack. Moreover, as we shall see later, sudden death causes one of the most traumatic and painful bereavements for the survivors.

Newsweek of September 14, 1964, reported on the reactions of Americans to this tragic death, and it is intriguing in the light of our discussion of Lindemann's work. The magazine found that this sudden death had produced a whole series of affects: shock and disbelief (what psychiatrists would term "denial"); then, with the acceptance of the fact of his death, there came a wave of feelings of sadness, sorrow, anger; some half of the people queried admitted suffering with crying, difficulties with sleeping, loss of appetite; more than two-thirds of the interviewees were tense.

Drs. Paul Sheatsley and Jacob Feldman studied a representative sample of Americans in a nationwide poll to test the affects of this assassination. Nine out of ten respondents suffered physical symptoms while two out of three felt nervous and tense. A majority were dazed and numb while most—men and women alike—cried at some point during the days immediately following the death. Most significantly, those responding to the poll compared Kennedy's death to that of a parent, relative or close friend.

I myself can still recall vividly the day I spent watching the funeral on TV—there was the clip-clop of the horses' hooves, the slow sorrowful beat of the music . . . but most of all there was a sort of numb feeling—I didn't know how long I was watching, nor the time the whole televised funeral had taken. When the day was over I suddenly realized I had neither dressed nor shaved—there was a state of benumbed confusion, and even now as I look back it is all a dull gray sort of thing with limited feelings still there, even though I recall I cried along with the multitudes lining the Washington streets through which the funeral cortege dolefully passed. This very numbness, as we shall soon see, is an important part of the first few days following the death of a meaningful or loved person.

So in these two major tragedies—the Cocoanut Grove fire and the president's assassination—we find the typical patterns of bereavement. The first was one in which the loss was a personal one (felt by members of the immediate family and the survivors), and the second was a national one which was taken as a very personal one and reacted to as such by the people of our nation as a whole. To understand this we must appreciate. . .

The Symbolic Nature of Mankind

In the presidential assassination we see how symbolism, the most uniquely human trait in mental activity, operates. Since much of what we will be discussing here depends on symbolism, we might say a word about it. Symbolism is essentially a secret language in which a symbol represents something else to which meaning has been attached by some person.

The symbol is often used to disguise the unacceptable, something with which the individual cannot cope psychologically, cannot deal with one-on-one as it were. For example, one young man who had undergone brain surgery dreamed for many months afterward of how he was beating someone over the head with a variety of objects but never hurting those he assaulted (say with a rubber hammer). He was saying symbolically that he hadn't had *his* head opened (the brain surgery), so he was instead doing it to someone else (a form of denial)—and that doing it didn't cause any damage anyhow.

In this way, body parts and family members are commonly dealt with symbolically—in a dream a sword or car may be used to represent the male sex organ (a phallic symbol) while the president or a general (an authority figure, too) may be used to represent the father or parental image.

The Kaleidoscope of Grief

The bereaved person goes through sensations and affects as vastly different, as rapidly changing and ever-shifting as the patterns and colors in a kaleidoscope. Intimate details will come in the particular chapters, while here we look only at the big picture, touch on the general things a mourner may experience so that there is no fear at these bizarre occurrences. Bereaved persons have told me they even doubted their own sanity temporarily as these feelings and emotions and sensations took possession of them. Just the knowledge that these experiences are perfectly normal is vastly reassuring to the bereaved.

In the perfectly normal and usual grief of the acute stage—say up to six months or so and possibly even a year—many things can and do happen. Grief is highly individual, so it's impossible to predict or describe exactly what any particular person will experience. However, the broad general patterns that Lindemann described can be anticipated although there is a wide and very individual variability in details.

The bereaved are caught in wild, uncontrollable crosscurrents of irrational and opposite feelings which come rolling over them in successive and unpredictable ways. Immediately after the loved one dies, there is shock and even disbelief, along with a numbness by means of which Nature fortunately protects the sufferer through those first and most terrible hours or days. Despite this numbness there may be weeping or wailing, but this initial reaction lasts only a short time ("I was completely numb that first week after my husband died," as one widow told me). Agitation is common and sleep may be difficult and when it does come is a restless, confused kind.

The acute stage of grief (actually the second stage, after the initial reaction we described above) can last three to six months, and only then does the sufferer begin to find some relief. The healing process—grief is like an illness or a wound—is slow and painful, as after surgery. It is during this second stage that the worst anguish of grief is felt; now that the numbness and shock of the initial reaction have worn off, the full impact of the loss is felt for the first time. Any healing and recovery are not likely even to begin for at least one to two months and perhaps as much as six. And even when the recovery and healing do start, they follow an uneven pattern of ups and downs: "I felt fine for a few days and then I went under again" is typical of what one hears from those in this stage of grief.

These patterns of acute grief usually wear off in a year or so, although most experts feel the loss of a child produces a permanent bereavement in the parents, particularly the mother. During the acute stage a common complaint is loss of memory which often takes strange forms (not remembering how much was paid for certain things, for example). Insomnia is common, too, and the bereaved are likely to become night owls, unable to go to bed until long after midnight. Crying spells come on suddenly and eating habits are disrupted—there may be a loss of both appetite and weight, or a ravenous bolting of excessive food with a resultant enormous gain in both girth and pounds.

The bereaved, particularly in the early weeks or months, lose all interest in the world around them. One active church member didn't even attend Sunday services for many months. There may be lethargy, or an uncontrollable restlessness, along with an inability to concentrate on the work at hand.

But gradually as the first year after the loss wears on, the patterns change and stabilize. The sadness—so overwhelming and ever-present at first—begins to subside and the episodes of deep sorrow become both less frequent and less intense. The memories of the deceased—so terribly painful at first—change their character, and recalls of the past begin to gain shades of poignancy and are tinged with pleasantness, are finally even savored and enjoyed with humor. Normal activities, too, are slowly resumed (church services and committee meetings, for example, are attended once more).

At the start of mourning, guilt feelings are overwhelming as, typically, survivors attack themselves—why didn't they go to that concert when the deceased asked to, or why wasn't different medical care sought earlier, perhaps they might have saved the deceased's life by doing other things differently? But along with these guilt feelings there is intense anger—anger with the deceased for dying, anger with the world, anger that is readily turned on the physicians or surgeons (why didn't they do their jobs better?), even anger with God (ministers are very familiar with this and how virulent it can be).

This underlying anger is easily brought out and directed at anyone and anything on the slightest provocation—and can create a host of immediate and later problems. This is the reason for the intense fights that so commonly erupt at funerals, the clashes with family and friends which often end long and intimate relationships unless both parties are aware of the problems and have an understanding of the grief process. When the bereaved angrily demands, ''Why did he (or she) die and leave me?'' and turns the anger onto the deceased, this creates more guilt feelings for the mourner, even though it's a perfectly normal reaction.

This first year of mourning is a stormy one and filled with irrational thoughts and actions which somehow seem perfectly rational and logical to the mourner at the time. But the path slowly smooths itself out as the end of that year approaches and passes.

The first holidays and special events that occur after the death —birthdays, wedding anniversaries, Christmas and New Year's and so on—are times of especial unhappiness and disturbances. But by the time these roll around for the second time, there still will be sadness, but it's now a sadness tinged with nostalgia and gentleness rather than with all the hurt and anger and bitterness of earlier.

One of the most disturbing of all experiences for many mourners is the hallucinations that so many bereaved undergo, and studies indicate these are likely to happen to some half of America's bereaved. These may consist of sensations of being touched by the deceased, of feeling his or her presence in the room, hearing the voice of the dead person or seeing him or her standing there. The mourner's reaction can be severe if not prepared—''I thought I was losing my mind''—yet we now know this experience is perfectly normal and is felt to be helpful by many mourners.

Recent scientific work offers the possibility of both a new depth in our understanding and perhaps the development of novel and exciting forms of therapies. . .

The Biology and Biochemistry of Grief

That grief reactions are normal and come from deep within the human psyche is evident from the fact that in the animal world, too, we discover the equivalent of the human grief reaction to loss. Dr. Konrad Lorenz, Nobel Prize-winning zoologist, has reported how the gray goose, separated from its mate, will move restlessly about night and day, make long flights to places the mate might be, while continuously crying out and searching farther and farther away. Thus animals exhibit behavior that is typical of what we consider "human" grief. A female gorilla or monkey may carry the body of her dead infant for days as if denying its death—again, behavior similar to the human being's initial denial of death.

A monkey that has lost its mother will sit huddled up and by itself, will show no interest in the world about it. Those who deal with animals—dog breeders or zoo keepers—will tell you how their animals that have lost their mothers will behave in ways very similar to grieving humans. Those of us who have bred dogs, for example, are quite familiar with the grieflike behavior of the animal abandoned by its owner: the hangdog expression and stance are very much like the drooping head and the slumping shoulders of the newly bereaved human being.

Obviously the grieving of the human being is on a biological basis and goes far back into the evolutionary development of the animal, back into the distant mists of time where man himself evolved, many millions of years ago, from lower forms of animal life.

Dr. George L. Engel, University of Rochester professor of psychiatry and of medicine, reports that people who have lost significant others in their past can be provoked to a sadness at which point there is an actual change in their growth hormone levels. Dr. George H. Pollock—University of Illinois professor of psychiatry, former president of the American Psychoanalytic Association, director of the Chicago Psychoanalytic Institute—

reports recent biological studies that suggest that there are biochemical and even possibly neurophysiological changes that take place within the various stages of the mourning process.

The Promise of Grief

Dr. Pollock also offers a new and exciting concept of the mourning process which he conceives of as one where "this fundamental and universal process may be seen as the adaptation to loss and change with an outcome of resolution, gain, creativity, and/or investment in new areas, activities, ideals and objects."

In short to grieve can be to grow!

But now let us look at the physical damage that grief can do to mourners—and why so many experts insist grief is an illness.

CHAPTER TWO

The Broken Heart: The Illness That Is Grief

> To every thing there is a season, and a
> time to every purpose under the heaven:
> A time to rend, and a time to sew;
>
> Ecclesiastes 3:1,7

Grief was already an ancient problem when the Bible was still only forming in men's minds so it's not surprising that awareness of bereavement should be found in the Psalms. And grief does start with a rending—with a variety of physical symptoms and even a broken heart—which only slowly yield to the putting together, the sewing up of the wounds and the healing of the sickness that is bereavement. Yet the broken bone that has healed is often stronger than the original uninjured one.

But these frequently strange physical symptoms, the bizarre illness that is grief, can be disturbing and even terrifying, unless the mourner knows and recognizes the process for what it is and sees the signs for their real meaning. Once these are understood, however, there is no more fear, and the mourner can protect himself or herself from this illness which can then be allowed slowly to drift its usual way until the bereaved is whole again.

The process of grief and the course it follows are the same whether in the United States or England, in Wales or in Australia. So one can only assume that bereavement is basically the same everywhere. Any differences in normal bereavement arise from whether the death itself was sudden or long-awaited, whether the mourners are young or old, whether the relationship between deceased and survivor was that of parent and child, brother and sister, husband and wife.

The physical symptoms of grief are common to all bereavement, but if they are not recognized as being typical, they can be frightening. Knowing them when they appear is reassuring, as it was for me, and makes the process that much easier. Friends who have also grieved and to whom I've shown this chapter have read it and then simply shaken their heads and said as did one woman: "I know, I know—yes, how well I know." And a man said to me angrily: "Why didn't someone tell all this *beforehand* so I wouldn't have been so terrified, had so bad a time with it?" Here then it *is* told.

The Illnesses Caused by Grief

Mankind's healers—physicians or witch doctors or priests— have always blamed illnesses on grief which itself was even accepted as an official cause of death only a very few hundred years ago. And even in the last century many diseases were still being blamed on grief. The writers of the past have often seen bereavement as the cause of sickness. But the scientific age that was born with Pasteur turned to microbes and damaged hearts or strokes as the causes. Yet now, within the last half century, modern science has recognized that grief *is* a cause of illness, that somehow it's tied to many of our most deadly and frightening diseases, to cancer and heart attack and many of the rest as well.

The symptoms grief usually causes are essentially benign, disturbances which like grief itself pass without permanent damage. In fact this mourning process can and should leave the bereaved stronger than before this emotional and physical storm. So let us now look at the normal and seemingly universal phenomena that occur with grief. The psychological aspects we'll leave for our next chapter and in this chapter limit ourselves to the physical reactions alone. First perhaps we should ask . . .

Which Bereaved Are Affected, and Which Suffer the Most?

Since Lindemann's classic report some thirty years ago, there have been increasing numbers of studies on the varied facets of grief and bereavement. Many of these articles are concerned with the frequency and statistics of grief reactions ranging from illness and mortality to the emotional affects of the death of a loved one. The bulk of these have been concerned with widows, and to a lesser extent, widowers. Perhaps this is as it should be since the great majority of deaths are men and women who are husbands and wives, although these deceased people are also brothers and sisters, fathers and mothers and children as well.

There are probably two reasons why so much of the work on bereavement has been concentrated on widows. For one thing, three out of four American women will become widows, and there are some eleven million widows in the United States right now. And the other reason is that widows take a peculiar beating from their problem, as we shall see later, both emotionally and realistically.

How much of what has been found true among widows and widowers applies to the other bereaved, to children and siblings and parents and the rest? The results from a variety of studies—bereaved people in St. Louis, Missouri, in the small market town of Llanidloes (population, 2350) in Wales, widows and widowers, as well as others in London and Boston, in Sydney, Australia, and in the Bronx, in a broad United States study—all seem to indicate that whether in grief or not, people are still people, that grief is a deeply based human reaction which is universal in character.

While the symptoms of grief might seem to occur more frequently in women, except for crying there really is no scientifically and statistically significant difference between the sexes—nor does age seem to matter either, although there would appear only a difference in the ability to concentrate and perhaps in memory. But there is the question as to whether these problems weren't present before the bereavement in the aged. Nor does it seem to matter so far as the physical symptoms are concerned whether the loss is that of a spouse or of another relative—or whether the illness was a short or a long one.

However, there do appear differences where the death of the *bereaved* is concerned. For the increased mortality among those who have lost loved ones does vary in a number of respects. While a variety of close relatives are involved in this mortality, those who have lost spouses have higher death rates, and the bereaved men are affected more than the women. There is also a higher death rate among the bereaved young spouses than the older ones—and, as always, higher among the male of the species than the female (the widowers than the widows).

But what of the physical happenings in this disease we call grief?

The Signs and Symptoms of Grief

We've all seen people who've experienced losses or separations, if not actual bereavements, and we've all suffered these from birth onward. Stop for one moment, however, and think what happens when someone gets the shock of hearing bad news, or of a loss, say, or of the death of a loved one. It's there in literature and drama and ordinary everyday life—the person suddenly turns weak and may even collapse as the legs give way.

Let's look now at this on a lesser scale, not, say, the death of a loved one but when someone dear goes off on a trip, moves away, is drafted into the armed services or given a foreign assignment for several years. Under these circumstances the moment of separation will usually cause no collapse, but instead the shoulders will sag, the face fall, the person will slump forward and perhaps sigh very deeply. And there is now evidence that biochemical changes, too, take place in the body during grief and mourning.

The pattern that the human being goes through in grief was first described by Lindemann in his 1944 article. He saw in the bereaved he studied an almost uniformity of reaction. There would be a tightness of the throat and a dryness in the mouth; waves of physical distress would sweep over the sufferers and might last for anywhere from twenty minutes to an hour at a time. There would be pronounced sighing as the bereaved breathed, along with a certain choking and shortness of breath. There was a loss of muscular strength (as one athletic woman put it to me: "My legs just don't seem to be able to hold me up") which clearly is at the basis of the collapsing and sagging mentioned above. There's an empty feeling in the stomach, a sensation perhaps of "butterflies in my stomach" and an inability to eat (as I've been told: "I have to stuff any food down"; "Food has no taste for me"; "It all tastes like sawdust").

In investigations covering some 150 bereaved individuals, Dr. Paula J. Clayton, University of Washington (St. Louis) professor of psychiatry, found that the most common physical problem was sleep disturbance (as I have heard the bereaved say: "I just can't sleep"; "I don't want to go to bed until I can no longer keep my eyes open"; "I can't bear to wake up to face the morning so I sleep late") and the next most frequent was crying. The Harvard Bereavement Study (only recently reported in the book, *The First Year of Bereavement* by Ira C. Glick and others) found that 92 percent of Boston widows they interviewed cried when reacting to the death. And Dr. Clayton found that 85 percent of those in a group of St. Louis bereaved were troubled by sleep disturbances within the first two weeks or so of their loss; 79 percent reported crying, while virtually half suffered loss of appetite and some also lost weight.

But despite the frequency of these problems they still only represent the tip of the iceberg of the full gamut of physical effects of grief. The universality of these problems is clear from a report by Dr. David Maddison, University of Sydney professor of psychiatry, and Agnes Viola. This team found that among the widows they queried in both Boston and in Sydney, Australia, there were few symptoms that differed significantly in these communities some eight thousand miles apart and separated by half the globe.

The most common physical symptoms of grief, Maddison found, were insomnia, a reduced capacity for work, and gross fatigue. Among the more common ones were trembling, headache, blurred vision, dizziness, excessive sweating and skin rashes, indigestion, difficulty in swallowing, weight loss and weight gain, vomiting and loss of appetite as well as excessive appetite, heart palpitations and chest pain, shortness of breath, general aching, excessive bleeding during menstrual periods, and asthma. And Dr. Clayton found constipation and frequent urination are also common symptoms of grief.

The personal stories the bereaved have to tell are not surprisingly different and can be summed up: ''I was frightened by the chest pains I had after ——— died.'' ''My hands trembled and my knees shook; I'd stammer.'' ''I always seemed to have trouble catching my breath.'' ''It seemed as if I was panting all the time.'' ''I couldn't stop eating.'' ''I'd stay up late and then just eat cake and ice cream and whatever else I could find in the refrigerator.'' ''I just seemed to put on weight by leaps and bounds.'' ''I couldn't eat—everything tasted like sand and nothing looked good to me. I had to choke the food down just to get some in and I lost a lot of weight.'' One widow had a severe skin rash and her face was swollen: diagnosed as ''allergic,'' the dermatologist admitted it was really due to her grief. A bereaved dentist was plagued with headaches and bothered by dizziness.

The Harvard study found that widows suffered such physical problems as these within hours of the death of their husbands and

these symptoms often multiplied and became exaggerated following the funeral. Frequently the symptoms of the disease that killed
the husband would appear (chest or arm pains in the wives of those
dying of heart attacks, for example); generalized aches and pains
were commonly accompanied by feelings of fatigue and of oncoming illness. The most disturbing problems of all were the sleep
disturbances. I avoided bed until after three in the morning, only to
waken within twenty minutes with the memory of disquieting
dreams involving my brother. A writer I know had difficulty
staying awake during the day and lost lots of time sleeping during
the early weeks of his bereavement, leaving him furious with
himself.

But slowly as the first couple of months pass, these symptoms
usually disappear by fits and starts. Gradually the mourners move
closer and closer to normal for longer and longer periods. After six
months or so, a good part of the time is bearable if not exactly
comfortable, and by the end of the first year or so the bereaved
person is usually going along at a fairly steady pace with many of
these physical symptoms either gone or at least so smoothed out
that ordinary life and functioning are no longer seriously interfered
with. We'll discuss this timetable in detail in chapter 6, "The
Time Frame and Determinants of Grief. . . ." But now let's see
about . . .

Always the Promise

A return to a sufficient degree of normality, to a point where
active functioning and full participation in life are routine, is
usually achieved over a period of one or two or three years. Most
say, however, that a mother never ceases grieving for a lost child
and to a lesser degree that this is also true for the widow's grief for
her dead husband. However, life can offer pleasure and fulfillment
even to these, as we shall see. Many looked back and I've often

heard either this remark of a friend or some minor modification of it: "I just don't know how I lived through it all." Yet almost all bereaved people manage—but not all, for grief can bring illness and even death for some.

Yet many do come through this experience stronger, more understanding and richer human beings. Just how much any particular person can grow with his or her grief will determine how much he or she can turn loss into gain, suffering into strength.

But what specifically are . . .

The Illnesses of Grief

Folk wisdom has since the dawn of history known that loss of a loved one can and does cause illness. Only now, however, do we have statistical proof. With our modern understanding of "stress," we have an acceptable scientific explanation of how this process may well work.

There are a number of diseases that seem to be closely involved in bereavement, sicknesses that may actually be caused by grief. In short, the ancient "Grief will make you sick" is another of those truly wise folk sayings. A half century ago, Dr. Walter B. Cannon, great American physiologist and pioneer in the role of the emotion in bodily functioning, was studying the role of stress (which we shall discuss very shortly). In 1929 he reported how a disorder of the thyroid gland developed in a woman whose husband committed suicide.

Next came a reported connection between asthma and bereavement. And Lindemann studied eighty-seven patients hospitalized for ulcerative colitis—seventy-five of these proved to have suffered a major separation before their illnesses started. Other investigators gradually recognized that a wide range of disease appeared to be tied to bereavement and separation. These disorders include such seemingly disparate conditions as a condition of overproduction of thyroid hormone (believed due to stress), ulcerative colitis, asthma and eczema, peptic ulcer, rheumatoid arthritis and osteoarthritis, diabetes, tuberculosis, a variety of heart diseases and hypertension (high blood pressure)—and even a number of cancers. Very often, too, chronic diseases such as arthritis are worsened during this time.

Just why grief should show itself in certain people in particular diseases is not fully understood, and we will discuss a possible answer when we talk about stress later in this chapter. However, vast amounts of research are being directed at this problem, and some answers are likely to be found in the not-too-distant future. Closely related to this is another problem.

Hypochondriasis and Grief

One widow I've spoken with can recall nighttime panics during her bereavement when she was sure she had cancer or had suffered a heart attack or whatever. And a recent widower was certain he had a brain tumor each time he suffered a tension headache. Hypochondriasis itself is a preoccupation with one's general physical health or that of certain specific body organs. The hypochondriac may often be disturbed by feelings the rest of us ignore, or he or she may magnify perfectly normal sensations. Often the person's true problem (such as separation anxiety) is hidden and becomes expressed in bodily complaints.

Hypochondriasis may be a passing stage in grief so that arthritic arm pains are believed to signal a heart attack, constipation to indicate an intestinal cancer, or those we just mentioned in the last paragraph. Typically the widow whose husband died of a heart attack will complain of the chest or arm pains that marked her spouse's fatal attack. While hypochondriasis is a symptom of an emotional problem and benign from a physical point of view, there is one effect of grief which certainly is not.

Hypochondriasis, Grief and Loss: An Answer to the Mystery?

One must always retain perspective—recognize that the vast majority of those who suffer grief and go through bereavement, and everyone will at one time or another, come through the other side, recover and go on in pretty much the same physical state in which the pain and agony of the grief began. In fact, if one takes advantage of the opportunity for growth and change that grief provides (we will discuss this as we go along), then one can end up stronger and more mature, even a happier person.

However, sometimes serious illness does happen in bereavement, and we may even find here at least one answer to the strange mystery that is cancer. Dr. Lawrence LeShan, New York psychologist, has done some of the intriguing early work into the unique personality structure of the cancer patient, an approach that has been attracting the attention of many investigators for a considerable time now.

Dr. LeShan says that even Galen (a Greek physician of the early first century A.D. and one of the greatest ancients) suspected that depressed women were more susceptible than cheerful ones. More than ninety years ago an American surgeon recognized "grief" as particularly linked to breast cancer, while an English physician a few years later noted that some two-thirds of a series of cancer patients had experienced recent bereavements.

Thus was clearly foreshadowed the recent work of a medical team at the University of Rochester where these physicians hold joint professorships in medicine and psychiatry. Over a fifteen-year period, one of the doctors—William A. Greene—studied a hundred adults with blood cancer (either leukemia or lymphoma). With only a half-dozen exceptions, these cancers appeared when the patient was suffering from either a real or feared loss (bereavement is only one form of loss or separation, but being a permanent kind it has a more severe impact).

Even the cancer patient relapses that Dr. Greene observed

coincided with a loss. Take one of Greene's patients: a woman with a blood cancer, she suffered a serious relapse after a three-year remission—just before her son entered the armed services, and then later this woman had another relapse when her older son was recalled to service.

Another woman developed breast cancer and underwent surgery following a pair of losses—the accidental crippling of her husband (we'll see later how this can produce grief) and the marriage of her daughter. Five years later this same woman's son was drafted, and a second cancer now sent her back into the hospital. And in a study of nearly two dozen men with leukemia and lymphoma, Dr. Greene also found that the diseases showed themselves in almost all instances when the men were suffering a loss or separation from a significant person (commonly a mother or mother figure and typically by a death).

This Rochester medical team believes that important factors in these diseases are the feelings of helplessness or hopelessness that these subjects had—what the Rochester group formally terms "the giving up-given up complex." And it is here that one major value of this book lies—by recognizing the patterns of grief one is no longer overwhelmed or terrorized by it, one no longer feels helpless and hopeless before it, one need not give up but recognize instead that everyone else goes through these same feelings and symptoms, and recovers in the very nature of the bereavement process. If the Rochester medical team is correct, this proper attitude (*not* giving up, *not* feeling helpless or hopeless) might even protect people from the illnesses of grief.

As Dr. Greene explains about these people who do get ill, when the doctors talk with them at length, they finally say, "Well, after it happened I lost interest. I just had to push myself to keep going." In short, these people felt they were in a situation where their losses left them with a "this is the end of the line" sort of feeling.

But if people will recognize and use grief as an opportunity for growth and change, for a better richer life, then there will be no such feelings. And we will later explore the avenues that can be taken for this growth, the sources of help to which one can turn when one can't find these within oneself. Chapter 9 will suggest to whom one can turn for support, while the last chapter specifically discusses the road back and how to follow it.

But the reality and the problems are there, and only their recognition offers hope so we must probe . . .

The Broken Heart and the Mortality of Grief

Modern Americans tend to laugh at anything out of the past, for ours is a future-oriented society, one in which anything old is regarded as obsolete and useless, like the TV set of 1945 or a pre-World War I car. So it is that the yesteryear talk of people dying of a "broken heart" is laughed at. But the latest scientific studies seem to give this concept a startling new statistical validity. For the bereaved person, and particularly the young widower, is what doctors would call "a person at risk," namely, someone who is in a category where the rate of illness or mortality is exceptionally high.

We have already seen the increased likelihood of the bereaved person facing illness, but the frequently given and most widely accepted figures for the mortality of bereavement are startling. A report on a symposium on bereavement (in the *British Medical Journal* in 1967) indicates that widowers in the first six months following bereavement show a 50 percent increase in the number of deaths from heart attacks—straight "broken heart" stuff if you will!

Drs. Kraus and Lilienfeld, in a report based on all United States deaths of those twenty to seventy-four years of age, 1949 to 1951, found the death rates for the widowed consistently higher than those for married people—and higher for widowers than for widows. The death rate for young widowers is about double that for young widows. This increased mortality risk among the bereaved drops as the age of the bereaved increases. But men are always at greater risk than women, and the first six months particularly would seem to be the period of greatest danger.

This increase in mortality isn't limited to the widowed but includes other close relatives, as Dr. W. Dewi Rees and Ms. Sylvia G. Lutkins showed in the tiny Welsh market town of Llanidloes. Not only did the widowed have an increased mortality during the first two years of bereavement, but so did such close relatives as parents, children and siblings. Here, too, men were at greater risk, with female children the least.

Strangely, the risk was five times greater when the deceased died at some place other than home but only twice as great when the death took place in a hospital rather than at home. The deaths at these other sites (road, shop, field or whatever) were usually sudden and unexpected and so the shock was greater, and often increased by an autopsy and inquest. We will discuss this question of what kinds of death are most disturbing in our later chapters.

This ancient belief that grief can kill—and by a "broken heart"—has considerable modern proof, including a study by Dr. Colin Murray Parkes and associates of some 4500 British widowers, fifty-five years of age and older. The death rate during the first six months of bereavement was 40 percent higher than that expected for married men the same age. Later in the bereavement the bereaved rates gradually fell to the married level. But the greatest increase in mortality was in those who died from heart disease, the broken heart of antiquity.

But the question is why there should be increased physical illness and mortality among the bereaved, and what can be done to prevent and control this. First, though, let us look at one explanation which lies in a concept of the last half century.

Stress: Take It or Leave It?

Ours is an age of stress, for it's all about us: it goes with us in the streets where we walk today with fear; it's on the job where our tension inevitably rises; in the house we may clash with spouse or child or parent. But whether a person answers the phone to be told a loved one has died, or that he or she has won a million dollars, the result is the same: stress!

When you are stressed, your heart will pound, you'll breathe hard, your eye pupils dilate and your palms get sweaty, your stomach ties into knots and your digestion grinds to a halt: this is the face of stress. And if it all sounds familiar after what we've been talking about in this chapter on the physical side of grief, you're right. For grief, bereavement—the reaction to the death of a loved one—does produce stress. But in bereavement the stress lasts until the grief work has been done and the time needed for healing and recovery has passed.

Traditionally, people and doctors alike advise that we avoid stress: "You'll live longer that way!" But Dr. Hans Selye, professor and director of the Institute of Experimental Medicine at the University of Montreal and the world's foremost authority on stress, put it this way to me: "Freedom from stress is death—don't try to avoid stress—it's the very salt and spice of life! But do learn to master and to use it!" The very same can be said of grief—don't try to avoid its pain and torment or you will pay dearly for this avoidance in the form of inadequate or uncompleted grief.

Since stress may well give us insight into at least one mechanism whereby grief produces its physical effects, let us look at stress in a compressed but thorough fashion. The word "stress" is limited by experts such as Dr. Selye and physicians to those bodily responses (the physical such as sweating, the psychological such as emotional tension, and the hormonal such as adrenalin poured into the blood) that take place when the individual is confronted by changes or challenges. This response—the "stress reaction"—is nonspecific, and is the same whether the stressful life event or "stressor" is good or bad, the death of a loved one or the sudden good news.

This response was first recognized by Dr. Walter Cannon when, in his classic book of some half century ago, he explained the bodily changes that go with pain, hunger, anger and fear—his famous "fight or flight" reaction. Pouring adrenalin into the bloodstream from its adrenal glands prepares the animal for survival by bringing it to its peak either for fighting back or for running away.

This adaptive reaction prepares the body for emergencies: sugar pours into the blood for quick energy; heavy breathing provides more oxygen and gets rid of extra carbon dioxide from intense activity; muscles tense for maximum effort; the heart speeds up and blood pressure rises to get fuel and oxygen around the body; digestive processes are brought to a halt so as not to interfere; and even the senses become sharper (eye pupils dilate so that more light enters and nothing is missed). If you're surprised that so much of this bodily change sounds like what happens to the grieving person, don't be, for grief is a stressful event and the body knows only one way to react to stressors.

But with modern human beings this fight-or-flight mechanism sometimes does damage: where it once protected primitive man in the wild jungles, it now sometimes acts when it's really not useful. Such a physical reaction does not help when you're faced with a tax return or with grief, and when stress becomes chronic or long lasting, it can lead to a whole range of so-called "stress diseases."

Dr. Selye sees stress in terms of his "general adaptation syndrome" which consists of three stages:

1. Alarm reaction—the brain sends a biochemical messenger to trigger the pituitary gland to send a hormone to the adrenal gland to produce adrenalin and other hormones. It is the adrenalin and

related hormones that produce the fight-or-flight body changes. Should the stressor be overwhelming (severe burns, for example), the victim, if you will, may succumb and finally die.

2. Resistance stage—if the stressor is not overwhelming, resistance develops and the body repairs the damage while bodily signs of the alarm reaction disappear.

3. Exhaustion stage—if a stressor continues for a long time after adaptation, the body's irreplaceable "adaptation energy" (the capacity to adapt) is eventually exhausted and an irreversible alarm reaction occurs and the individual can die.

It is when the person is subjected to the original stressors during the exhaustion stage that the so-called "stress-related" diseases appear—such disorders as ulcerative colitis, rheumatoid arthritis, hypertension and the rest which we have seen as occurring in the bereaved. In one study of air traffic controllers, a stress-filled job, it was shown that hypertension, diabetes and peptic ulcers arose several times as often as in those with a related but much less stress-filled occupation.

A study of accountants during the tax season revealed that from January to the April 15 tax deadline their cholesterol and blood-clotting times rose steadily to a peak—and it is the high level of these two factors that are thought to be major elements in heart attacks. In fact, many experts believe that stress plays a role in virtually every disease from the common cold to cancer, and there is surprisingly strong evidence to back up such a contention. Several leading physicians, for example, felt certain that former President Nixon's blood clots in leg and lung were due to stress, and they did occur only after his loss of the presidency.

Of considerable interest to the scientific medical community at this time is the work of Dr. Thomas H. Holmes, University of Washington (Seattle) professor of psychiatry, who in 1949 began keeping "life charts"—a sort of condensed life story—on more than five thousand patients. He found that certain life events seemed to bunch up in the period before major illnesses, and he made up a list of forty-three chief stressful life events. Holmes rated these in life units or points according to the degree of the problems the events created. Holmes feels that by adding the point score a person accumulates in the previous year one can tell one's danger of a major illness.

The top figure—100 points—is for "death of a spouse," followed by divorce, marital separation, jail term, death of close family member and so on down the line. The one theme that runs through the table is that of loss, separation or change—further evidence of the interrelationship between grief and stress and disease, of the ancient beliefs that grief causes people to sicken and even to die.

In the 1950s and '60s, Dr. Arthur H. Schmale, Jr., of the Rochester Group we discussed earlier, studied virtually two hundred patients treated at the University of Rochester Medical Center for infections, cancer, diseases of heart and blood vessels, rheumatoid arthritis, diabetes, diseases of the nervous system and so on. Some 80 percent of these people proved to have recently experienced a loss.

Even more startling, perhaps, was how Dr. Schmale and Dr. Howard P. Iker, also of this group, simply interviewed fifty-one women suspected of having cervical cancer. Before a biopsy was performed these two doctors tried to predict what the biopsy would show—by the stress these women had suffered and their feelings of hopelessness. Of the eighteen women the doctors anticipated to have cancer, eleven *did* have it. And of the thirty-three predicted to have *no* cancer, twenty-five did *not* have it!

Very recently, Dr. Vernon Riley of Seattle's Northwest Research Foundation, reported that some of the experimental mice kept there in the usual laboratory surroundings developed breast cancer 90 percent of the time (according to the *Journal of the American Medical Association*). By markedly reducing the animals' stress (cutting down on background noise, drafts and frequent handling), the incidence of cancer was brought down to a mere 7 percent of the time.

All of which opens the way to considering how one goes about . . .

Protecting Oneself

It's clear that if one is bereaved one is at risk, that there is greater danger of physical illness and worse than the average nonbereaved person. So the mourner is wise to seek a prompt medical consultation should there be any question as to health, any symptoms or physical problems (say chest pains or whatever). Statistically this is even more vital if the bereaved person is a man. In fact, a routine medical examination following bereavement is a wise measure, for it can not only catch any health problems early enough to correct or help them, but it can also relieve the underlying anxiety that these symptoms of illness so common in grief set off in virtually everybody.

Another interesting theory has arisen from the Rochester Group's work. As we have seen, they emphasize the danger of the giving-up attitude under stress, the threat of the hopeless and helpless feelings. So if the person who has just lost a loved one also has any of this sort of attitude, medical consultation becomes particularly important, since bereavement carries this extra danger of physical illness. Sometimes, too, a more specialized form of help is advisable if the grief process doesn't follow a healthy normal pattern—and this is what our next two chapters are all about—the "good grief" and the "grief work" that must be done, along with the inadequate mourning that causes trouble.

There are many professionals today who can help, from the better-trained family doctors to the modern minister who is skilled in counseling, and backing these up are the psychiatrist, the clinical psychologist and the psychiatric social worker.

In any case, the mourner should protect himself or herself. Even just understanding the physical aspects of grief will help mourners to grow and understand, to help others in turn with their problems—and it's long been known that helping others ultimately helps the helper most.

But now for the psychological side of grief.

CHAPTER THREE

Grief Work: Healing Through Good Grief

Blessed are they that mourn:
for they shall be comforted.

Matthew 5:4

"Grief work" (a term first used by Freud) is just what it says, the task of mourning. And it *is* work—hard, long, painful, slow, repetitive, a suffering through of the same effort over and over. It's a matter of rethinking and refeeling, reworking the same long-past fields, the same old emotional material, over and over—breaking through the denial and disbelief that the past and the deceased are both dead; reëxamining one's past life repeatedly and seeing each thought, each intimate experience, with and without the deceased, looking at everything that has gone before from a thousand or more points of view until finally the past like the deceased is ready to be buried. Out of all this a whole new mourner emerges with new attitudes, new concepts, new values, new appreciations of life itself; and if these *are* better than the old, then there has been growth and change and all the suffering has been worthwhile, then the grief has been good.

This is work whose rewards are the most precious in life, for only through this grief can a human being hope to learn really to live, to be able to face the human life of constant loss and separation, to face and make the most of life and age and even death, to add life to one's years instead of merely years to one's life.

48

Through grief one can learn to enjoy life to its fullest, and how to turn loss into gain.

The Challenge of Change: Grief into Growth, Loss into Gain

Without successful grief work (good grief, if you will), there can be no maturation or change, for there is no growth without grief, no gain without loss. Promotion to a new and better job means giving up the old familiar comfortable one; buying a bigger, nicer house involves getting rid of the old one; acquiring new skills and abilities calls for losing the old habits and knowledge. Even writing this book has been a painful growth experience, for it necessitated letting go of lifetime ties to my brother (less than six months dead), doing the necessary grief work so I could talk (write if you will) of these things—and as we shall see, this is successfully accomplishing the work of mourning, although it will surely be a long time before it has been fully completed.

We must talk of the two-sided coin, the ambivalence, of loss and grief—painful and tearing on one side, rich and happy with the fruits of new, different, more active patterns on the other. This must be dealt with successfully by the teenager before he or she can give up the protection of childhood, to venture into a new and frightening time from which he or she will then once more have to move as time continues to pass. It is painful and terrifying, which is why he or she moves forward into a near-adult one minute and runs back to the shelter of parent and childhood the next, torment both to himself or herself and the parents who must deal both with their child's problems and their own, for the maturing of the child signifies their own aging.

Childbirth too is involved here, for the pregnant young woman who hasn't learned to deal with loss and change is likely to suffer postpartum depression—the "childbirth blues," which are simply a reaction to the loss of the life the mother has carried within her for nine months and has now lost. However, this is more complex, and we will deal with it further in chapter 8.

If the older person hasn't done his or her grief work all along the way and learned to cope with grief and loss, then retirement and aging can be terribly traumatic with their losses and changes. And this failure to come to grips with grief is very likely at the roots of the illness and even death that is so commonly seen to follow on the heels of retirement. To grow old gracefully and successfully, too, as we shall see, is also a matter of learning to grow and change through grief work.

But now let us look at the big picture which we have only been touching on so far.

Grief—Its Psychological Side

Where grief and bereavement are concerned, the psychological side is the basis of the human reaction, the bottom line if you will, for the way people respond to the loss of a loved one is fundamentally psychic (with our minds and emotions). Recall for a moment the discussion of stress in the previous chapter—for the whole phenomenon starts with a message from the mind to the pituitary gland to set off the hormonal explosion that finally results in all the physical changes needed to prepare the body for fight or flight.

When you get "uptight" or "tense," it is because your muscles are contracting, on the orders, ultimately, of your conscious or unconscious mind. When, for example, you feel you're carrying too much of a load (symbolically), too many problems, then your head, neck and shoulder muscles are likely to tighten up as if they were dealing with a real and heavy pack to be carried. Should these muscles finally go into spasm from long-lasting contraction, then you get a headache (tension headaches are due to such muscle spasms).

Your psyche can also cause your stomach to secrete too much acid (in normal amounts it's needed for digestion) too often, until this eats a hole in your stomach's lining and you get a "peptic ulcer." Or your psyche can step up the normal muscular action of your intestines by which your food is moved along for digestion to be carried out and any useless material and waste products finally to be expelled. Should this muscular action be stepped up to the point where it becomes painful, you have what doctors today term the "irritable colon syndrome" (what was once called "spastic colon" or "mucous colitis"). Victims of this can suffer excruciating abdominal pain along with either diarrhea or constipation. As we saw in the last chapter, intestinal problems and headaches are common among the bereaved.

Thus the psychological side of grief can show itself in such physical complaints as "I felt too full to eat a thing," or "I seemed to have a lump in my chest," or whatever. But the question the bereaved are always concerned with in all their pain and turmoil is . . .

"How Permanent Is All This?"

The thoughts and emotions that sweep over the bereaved form a wild, disordered kaleidoscope—bizarre and haunting, coming on night and day, during waking and sleeping hours, plaguing and frightening mourners both by the seemingly "unnatural" character and the fact that the bereaved find they have no control over the fantastic feelings they experience. To make matters worse for those who know little of the nature of grief, there is a strange, alien, unfamiliar character to the feelings—ordinarily kindly and gentle people can turn even on those they love with violent uncon trollable rages, verbally attack friends or helpers such as ministers and doctors.

This is why reading about all this is so important, painful as it may be. For if this book is truly important and meaningful to the reader, he or she *will* find it uncomfortable to read, for it will touch on unhealed wounds which must be explored to permit the healing of good grief. Writing this during the first six months of my own bereavement, with wounds just beginning to heal, has been painful for me, and yet it has helped, as I hope it will help others, by exploring unhealed areas and so speeding their healing.

The importance of having this knowledge can be found in the remark of a hardheaded businessman who expressed to me some of the fears that haunted him through his mourning period: "I was terrified that I was really losing my grip, going right out of my mind . . . that I'd never be the same again, that I couldn't hope to operate my business, for I was doing things all wrong. . . . I didn't dare admit even to my own wife that I didn't know what the future held for me."

Yet this man need not have feared, for Sigmund Freud, some sixty years ago, made it clear that mourning is a natural process, normal and not pathological. Not only is medical treatment unwarranted, but any interference with healthy mourning is either useless or downright damaging. It does subside with the passage of time. Only recently, Dr. Clayton—in a follow-up interview of bereaved persons as little as one to four months after the death— found that 81 percent reported that their symptoms were improved, dating from some six to ten weeks after their loss, while another 15 percent felt better even though there was no improvement in symptoms.

It is enormously helpful for the bereaved to know that despite the terrible time they are having they will recover spontaneously and without medical or psychiatric help, in most instances. The symptoms and disturbances of grief *do* subside by themselves with time, and grief does follow certain broad patterns.

The Patterns and Time of Grief

Dr. Parkes, the British psychiatrist already mentioned and internationally known for his research in bereavement, believes that the most characteristic aspect of grief is its strangely acute and episodic nature—the "pangs of grief" with their painful anxiety, the terrible sense of loss and the sudden sobbing or crying out loud of the bereaved.

Nor does grief have a precise timetable or an exact pattern, for it's an ongoing process and not an incident like, say, a cut arm or a broken leg which doctors can predict just how long repair will take and the bleeding stop, or the time of healing. One can't say grief will take so many weeks to heal, after which we can remove some psychic cast; it is no simple disorder in which an X-ray shows healing and tells when the victim can start walking, working, playing tennis.

On the contrary, grief is a process in which healing best occurs as part of a gradual change and growth in the individual, a process of fits and starts, of episodes, if you will, during which the bereaved often relapse unpredictably into the earliest and most painful stages of the process.

In fact, this strange process might be compared to a man saying farewell to a loved one boarding a ship for a life on a distant shore. As the traveler boards ship, the relative on the dock waves farewell. Feelings of sorrow and loneliness, emptiness and hurt, grow as the ship pulls away. Tears come to the relative's eyes and he waves, tries still to make out the traveler on the ship's deck.

Finally the relative turns from the dockside with tears and hurt and slowly drifts away as the ship moves slowly from the shore. The watcher walks and waves, tries once more to make out the voyager and to remember him, finally turns his back on the ship. With drooping shoulders he moves another few feet, stops and repeats the waving, the peering, the tears, until eventually the end of the dock is reached, the ship is now barely visible in the distance. The memories, though, keep coming back, but the finality and permanence of the parting must now be accepted. However, even though as time passes, the memories and sorrow will still return on occasions: a birthday or holiday, some special time or place, perhaps.

This, too, is what happens in grief as slowly and reluctantly the bereaved separates from the loved one who has died. It's a gradual process, not a sudden cutting of ties, and it is only slowly that one is able to let go. The work of grief takes time, as much as a week for the initial reaction, six months or so for the very acute stage, and one, two, three years to complete the grieving. Reactions, however, continue afterward and some are said to be permanent, depending on the relationship to the deceased (husband, wife, child, sibling, parent, friend) and the way it all happened (suddenly, slowly, with knowledge beforehand, even suicide perhaps).

Now let us turn to this task of mourning and the detailed way in which it is carried out.

Grief Work: A Job to Be Done

We've used this phrase lightly and touched on its promise but not really looked at what must be done in this process, nor why it is so hard. To talk of grief work is to speak of the very stuff of life, the preparation for everything that's difficult and important and meaningful in life.

"Grief work" in the psychiatric sense was originally defined by Freud more than a half century ago. As he then explained, the task of mourning was the need for the individual to test reality, to prove to himself or herself that the loved one was dead (neither an easy nor a quick thing for humans to accept because the denial mechanism is one of the most powerful the human being must deal with in his or her psychic functioning), and then the survivor must cut all emotional ties to the dead person. Dr. Vamik D. Volkan, University of Virginia professor of psychiatry and one of America's leading experts on grief, puts it this way: "At the end of the grief work the bereaved person becomes gradually once more free and uninhibited to seek fresh attachments."

This is the specific role of grief work, but in the much bigger sense this process emphasizes the growth that is necessary to achieve the ultimate ends of freedom—to build a new life. To gain his or her freedom to grow, the bereaved must take advantage of grief work to reëxamine all the separations and losses in his or her life, to find a new meaning and a purpose in it all, to see his or her close relationships from this new perspective, and to recognize and admit the very finite limits of this existence, the need to make the most of the limited time man is given.

A grieving physician put it to me this way: "Everything looks different now—so much ceases to be important, and I understand what is really significant in life, in work and money and people and close relationships. My life will never be the same again." So it is that growth and creativity come out of grief, gain out of loss. Perhaps the most difficult part of the task is to accept the death and to recover one's emotional investment in the deceased so that we are free to put this to work in someone or something else.

But what can the bereaved expect in the various stages of grief? What psychic mechanisms are used and how do they affect the sufferer? How do distortions and strange emotional storms arise to toss the mourner about as the real Atlantic gales did the tiny ships of Columbus? Let us look at these three stages, beginning with . . .

The Initial Reaction—Those First Few Days

This is a period which no mourner can describe clearly, thanks to Nature's protective measures. Afterward, looking back, it is recalled as through a rolling mist which thins out occasionally to permit short glimpses of a distant blurred landscape, partly in sun and partly in blackest shadows. I think the closest thing to the initial stage of grief is the time immediately following major surgery when heavy doses of tranquilizing and pain-killing drugs combine with the physical and psychic shock of the operation to leave a confused half-life with flashes of terrible pain striking through the haze.

Nothing is precisely the same as the initial period of bereavement, those first few days or even the first week following the shock of the news of the death of a loved one. The event comes as a shock whether it was a sudden death in an accident or the result of a long-standing disease in which death has cast its shadow on the family for years with increasing and certain closeness.

Possibly the key word here *is* shock, for the bereaved are in a state of psychic shock during these first few days. It is thanks to this shock that the mourners can get through those first hideous few days. Many measures must be taken: to provide for and protect any small children, to contact relatives and close friends. There are hospital, medical and legal aspects (an autopsy either may be required or requested to help others eventually), and arrangements for funeral or cremation, burial or other disposition of the remains, any religious or other ceremonies. The husband of a dear friend of mine, for example, had to call and ask me, along with others, to speak at a Quaker-type funeral. My own brother wanted some things said not by a minister who barely knew him but by someone who cared and was close, who could say meaningful things, so I found myself speaking at two funerals barely a year apart.

The initial response on hearing the news or seeing it actually happen is invariably one of numb disbelief: "I don't believe it." When a call told me a very dear friend had died in a matter of minutes from a sudden heart attack, I gave an anguished, "Oh— no . . . it can't be." And as I write this less than three years later, the anguish still floods back—the tears, the terrible emptiness and the pain. As Dr. Volkan commented to me in our discussion not long after this friend had died: "Your friend will always live inside you," and he was right, for reasons which will be clear later in this chapter.

Mercifully, Nature covers the bereaved with a protective emotional blanket within minutes of the death news—there is a cold, empty numbness, a confused, dazed feeling of unreality that takes over. Thanks to this the mourners can get through this period with all that must be carried out. Also, the very worst and most acute of the pain has begun to subside before this cover wears thin, so that the slow process of healing has begun, to however slight an extent, before the disbelief must be dropped and the numbness gone, leaving the grieving to face the cold, terrible fact that the loved one is gone forever.

Dr. Parkes, too, has seen this same reaction, this first cry of great anguish before the blessed blanket of numbness descends within a few minutes. Survivors often wonder that they "have no feelings" when the death occurs; actually this is the normal numbness that moves so fast they're not even aware of the first reaction. As Parkes recalls, one widow in his London study of the first year of bereavement told him of this short-lived explosion: "I was aware of a horrible wailing and knew it was me. . . ." During this short moment before the numbness, there is almost a loss of contact with oneself and one sees oneself almost as if from a distance—and then the numbness, the cold, hard protection of unfeelingness almost, descends.

In this initial period there may be weeping or wailing; certainly there is a great deal of agitation. One widow I know commented wonderingly: "I don't feel anything, I don't cry or even talk about him—I'm just going about my usual work [she had her own career] and doing whatever has to be done." Only later do the bereaved realize how disturbed this period really was, how memory failed, things were mislaid or lost. Mrs. Lily Pincus, a British social worker and founder of the Institute for Marital Studies at London's famed Tavistock Institute, recalls how during those first numb days following her husband's death she picked up his important papers from his attorney—and threw them into a strange letter box.

During these first days, too, the individual may be lethargic or be overactive. Through the dull numbness—like lightning striking to light areas of blackness in a forest storm—there may be bursts of emotion, wailing or crying, periods when the numbness lifts briefly to let the feelings through, even momentarily to let in the awareness of the reality and the fact of death.

But all this takes only a matter of days, and the initial reaction, this bit of life virtually lost to the bereaved, passes—only to bring in its wake the realization and the terrible pain of . . .

The Second Stage of Grief

This is the most painful part of bereavement, for the protective numbness is gone and the sufferer must face the twin facts of death and of life (a life without the deceased and the relationship). With some, the initial numb stage may pass in hours or days, even a week or more. Then the acute stage begins, a period filled with moods that shift and change suddenly and unpredictably, more erratic, stormy, abrupt and unexpected than a summer shower. Waves of feelings sweep over the psyche already filled with guilt and anger, longing and anxiety, all at a time the psyche is struggling to incorporate the deceased into it, to accept this new situation.

While still trying to deny the death, the bereaved is simultaneously trying to accept the reality. Fighting against itself and against reality, angry at fate and God and the world for taking away the loved one, the mourner in this acute phase of his or her bereavement has to also deal with fears of insanity, for he or she is rocked by waves of uncontrollable anger. He or she has to face constant recollections of the past, hallucinations and dreams of the loved one, loss of memory (some go through periods in which they cannot even recall what the deceased looked like), a restless searching for the lost one and identifying oneself with the deceased (acting like the one who has been lost, for example).

There are efforts to rewrite one's life history to change the past relationships or what has happened or (wishful thinking, if you will). There is irritability and restlessness, an inability to concentrate and to sleep, too much eating or too little. There is a loss of interest in the world about (one man I know who was involved in politics didn't read the paper or vote for more than a year). There is loneliness and sadness—attacks of sheer panic occur at this time and waves of crying are readily precipitated.

But slowly through all this nightmare of emotion, healing begins haltingly. Yet this acute stage can last six or more months and is a time of serious potential problems which mourners should know about.

The Dangers of the Acute Stage of Grief

The only protection the bereaved really have here is knowledge, the awareness that they must not fully trust their own thinking. For they may think they're being entirely rational in their decisions and actions when actually they are totally irrational. Knowing this, one can protect oneself in case of bereavement simply by avoiding actions of any serious consequence. I rather suspected I was being irrational in buying a sports jacket and a color TV set the week after my brother's death, but I knew the mistake couldn't be a big one, so I went ahead. But I did avoid any more serious decisions and dealing with important situations.

Neither judgment nor thinking can be fully trusted during any of the three stages of grief. This includes both one's business activities and one's personal relationships. Many relationships—including marriages when a child dies—will break up for entirely irrational reasons during bereavement. This danger of errors in judgment extends even into the third stage.

The Third Stage of Grief: Beginning Recovery

Only after the first six months or so, when the acute grief has finally passed, does recovery really begin. But even then it is only a slow and halting process, moving by fits and starts. Some of the most discouraging and disturbing experiences in mourning are the relapses that occur. When the time comes, the bereaved does begin to feel better and to look ahead, returns to normal social activities and personal interests outside himself or herself, even reactivates the business involvements. The episodes of sadness are now less frequent and last for shorter periods; even the memories of the deceased are being recalled with nostalgia and some warmth and pleasure instead of just pain and sadness.

Yet just at this time of seeming recovery, there will suddenly be a relapse, spontaneously or with reason. It can be caused, perhaps, by an anniversary, some special holiday (Christmas and New Year's are particularly bad) or even a meaningful time or place from the past relationship.

Only by recognizing that there will be relapses—times when all the raw distress of the acute phase returns in full force—can the impact of such times be softened and the occurrence be drained of its frightening nature. But relapses, too, occur less and less often, have ever less force as the forces of healing become stronger with the passage of time and successful grief work.

How long does it all go on? This depends on the individual—for some the process may take a year, for others two or three. Under certain circumstances (the mother who loses a child, the woman who loses a husband), grief and bereavement may be virtually permanent.

How sharply defined and separated are the stages of grief? Not very, except for the first one with its limited affects, its numbness and total confusion. The other stages are like so much else about grief—a process and not an incident—and so are continuous and blend into one another. As a result it may be more helpful to explore this process by looking at the specific reactions that take place rather than concentrating on the stages. The first and frequently appearing ones include . . .

Denial, Disbelief and Searching

The first reaction to death is to disbelieve or deny—the way I reacted, for example, to my friend's death, "Oh . . . no . . ." Typical, too, is the "I don't believe it" one hears so often and later the same person may say, "I just can't believe he's dead. . . ." The Harvard Bereavement Study found that widows often reacted to news of a sudden accidental death with the feeling that the notification would prove to be a mistake in identifying the dead person, or that the diagnosis of death had been made too quickly and was simply a mistake.

The fact of death is often too much for the human psyche to cope with and so it must buy time, by denying the reality of death. This denial or disbelief really isn't a total thing, for just enough of reality is allowed to seep through so that the bereaved can slowly come to grips with the reality, can do the grief work and gradually accept the fact of death. Denial appears in many forms during the bereavement period, but when the work of mourning has been completed, the reality of the death is fully accepted. However, this acceptance does take time.

The restlessness of bereavement is believed by some to be a form of "searching," the kind of behavior we discussed earlier in which an animal—such as the gray goose—searches for its lost mate. This searching is a way of saying, "I'll find him—he's alive. . . ." Perhaps even the experience of thinking one sees the loved one—on the street or in a gathering or wherever—is a form of this searching, this denial of death. Denial is a powerful, human, psychic mechanism and disappears only slowly in grief, and the feelings of disbelief keep coming back. "It's three years now but it's still hard to believe that she's dead." Denial shows, too, in our dreams and even more strongly in a bizarre psychic way of dealing with death.

Hallucinations and Dreams

Hallucinations of the deceased may sound strange, terrifying, abnormal, outlandish, rare—feeling the touch of a hand now gone, the sound of a voice now stilled, the sight of one who is gone. Yet these hallucinations of the deceased are none of these; they are neither strange nor frightening nor abnormal nor even uncommon. Dr. Rees interviewed some three hundred widows and widowers in Llanidloes and found almost half had hallucinations of their dead spouses. Widowers had these illusions as often as widows, and the experiences often occurred over a period of many years but were most common during the first decade of widowhood. Young people were less likely to have this happen than those who had been widowed after the age of forty. The experience included those who simply felt the deceased to be present; those who saw the dead person, or heard him or her speak; who were touched by the deceased or spoke to them. Dr. Rees concluded—and other experts agree with him—that these hallucinations are ''normal and helpful accompaniments of widowhood.'' The bereaved involved mostly felt helped by the experience and it happened to people irrespective of their race or creed or sex. It has been found to happen among half of London widows—and 90 percent of Japanese ones.

This is obviously nothing new, for Robert Burton back in 1621 described this same phenomenon and even quoted classical sources of it in his *The Anatomy of Melancholy*. Dr. Parkes tells of a widow who saw her husband sitting in a chair on Christmas Day. And Dr. Peter Marris (one of England's leading sociologists) found that half the London widows in his study reported hallucinations, such as the widow who heard her husband cough and spoke to him; a widower who saw his wife sitting in a nearby chair while he was watching TV (one of the few who was disturbed by a hallucination, he fled the room and never entered it again). I know myself of several who either experienced similar illusions or knew those who did. Generally these seem to be comforting experiences, and many feel pleased that the deceased is in the house with them.

The Harvard Bereavement Study also found this common, and among Boston widows one reported talking long and loud to the deceased; another heard her dead husband coming home from work and putting his key in the lock; others saw the husband sitting reading his paper, even standing by the door. The Harvard Group concluded that one reason for the persistence of these hallucinations was simply that the experiences were comforting and not disturbing. Some of the widows even deliberately produced the illusions when they were particularly depressed because it relieved their sense of loneliness.

Dreams, too, occur widely, with Dr. Parkes finding that half the widows reported dreaming of their dead husbands, and again the dreamed experiences, most often, were not disturbing but happy instances of interaction with the deceased (talking or even arguing with the dead husband). However, Parkes always found that reality tended to force itself to some degree into the dream. And then there is always the end, the sad awakening. But now for the problems in grief.

Guilt and Anger

Irrational feelings of guilt and anger come and go in waves during bereavement, behave in strange ways. As the first six months and then the initial year pass, these feelings finally fade away, although they can leave serious damage in their wake, as we shall see. The feelings of the bereaved, however, are a confused, ambivalent mixture of opposites—and the more this is so, the more guilt and confusion are present.

Guilt shows itself in both rational and irrational thoughts: perhaps if I had taken him or her to a different hospital or doctor, I might have saved his or her life . . . if I had listened to what he or she said and gotten earlier care . . . did I do things properly or was there a better way . . . and so the thoughts go. These guilt feelings often have no basis in reality whatsoever, may even arise because of a supposed failure many years earlier (not getting the Sunday papers, or not going to a movie the deceased had wanted to see . . . not calling home more often during the day). In short the bereaved are filled with guilt which is usually irrational but slowly subsides as time passes and a more rational perspective finally takes over once more.

The guilt may even be based on feelings of anger and hostility for the deceased, or of unconscious death wishes such as a child feels toward parents (perfectly normal, in fact) or simply due to the moments when the bereaved is happy he or she was the one who survived. But it is the underlying anger which produces severe guilt—and there almost always is ambivalence—a love-hate relationship—felt toward people who are close (parents, siblings, child, spouse).

Anger too grows out of the very bereavement, anger so overwhelming over the fact of the loss that it spreads to touch physicians, friends, family, employers and employees, virtually anyone and everyone who enters the picture, including the minister and God as well. This can cause serious problems, for it leads to the many violent arguments at funerals, the irrational verbal attacks on others that have broken parent-child and other family relationships, marriages and lifelong friendships. Looking back to my own father's funeral many years ago, I know that this was the real cause for my violent clash with an uncle (we didn't speak for years afterward), and only my awareness of this problem (from my work on this book) saved me from many other clashes in these last six months.

There is no better evidence of the irrationality of this enormous illogical anger that the bereaved feel than the fact that this anger is so often felt toward the deceased. This is often outwardly based on the supposed fact that the deceased failed to care for himself or herself better or more successfully, or that the deceased contributed in some deliberate way to his or her own demise.

Parkes's study of London widows led him to suggest that two things play a role in this anger: the insecurity and the frustration that these survivors feel as a result of the loss of their chief source of support, along with the desire to gain some degree of control over the disinterested and impersonal nature of death. Frustration and a feeling of helplessness always produce anger so that such feelings, engendered by the death of a loved one, are bound to lead to anger and aggressive behavior, such as picking fights.

But time does heal all, and both anger and guilt fade by themselves as the individual carries out the task of mourning, his or her grief work, and slowly comes to peace with himself or herself. In part, too, the mourning period is concerned with . . .

Memories and Forgetfulness

Typical is the ambivalence of this confused time: "My bereavement is still only a confused, distant and dimly remembered time to me," as one bereaved person told me. This remark fits the feelings of most who have suffered through grief, with the only real difference being the length of time, whether a year or two or three. No better example of this ambivalence can be found than the constant remembering and reviewing of each circumstance leading up to the death and of the death itself, perhaps just the notification, since the bereaved may have been away from the hospital at the time.

Yet side by side with this detailed frequent recall go the difficulties with memory. Actually the separation anxiety created by the loss may be so great that it interferes with a good deal of intellectual functioning and so one's memory suffers. It is particularly in new things, Dr. Ewald W. Busse, Duke University professor of psychiatry, explains, that the bereaved "may find they don't learn as readily—they get preoccupied with their own problems rather than absorbing new things." In short the grieving person may not be able to remember how much he or she paid for something just bought or what a friend's new telephone number is, where ordinarily it would be easy to do so.

Sometimes too the anxiety is so high that it interferes with the ability to concentrate and think as well as remember, and this causes additional distress, for the sufferer may then fear what is happening to his or her mind. I, for example, have always carried things in my mind; I never write down what I have to do during the day (whom I have to call, what I have to write—letters, articles, whatever) or when. During the early part of my own bereavement I discovered I couldn't remember the myriad details I always handled without trouble. I had to resort to writing them down, but I wasn't accustomed to looking at notes, so that didn't help very much either. But as with others, my memory has come back fully, but it was six weeks or more after the death before it did, and it troubled me again at Christmastime and again at the time of my brother's birthday.

But the constant recall of the sad events—almost like an attempt to rewrite this bit of history, to make it come out differently by reliving it—is carried out in minute detail at the same time as other things can't be remembered. This very forgetting is used to protect the bereaved in a number of ways.

By selectively forgetting certain things, the pain of grief can be reduced. One widow could not recall the face of her dead husband during the first weeks of her bereavement. Another who had lost her husband some three years before still finds it hard to recall him when things are going badly and she is disturbed. In this way the psyche limits the disturbing situation of loss to what it can comfortably bear.

Another use of forgetting is to avoid the bad aspects of the deceased's character. One man told me how during the early weeks of his bereavement he couldn't recall a single bad thing about his father or their relationship. A woman who had failed to do her grief work was still talking of how perfect her mother was six years after the parent's death, even though the reality was quite different as she herself had told it before the death.

The bereaved who use this mechanism aren't really forgetting or trying deliberately to make saints out of abusive, arrogant, hostile or alcoholic people who have died; they're just trying to protect themselves against the anger and guilt they unconsciously feel about the reality of the deceased. As healthy bereavement wears on, this idealization tends to disappear and the bereaved person is finally able (if the grief work is successful) to see the dead in a wholly realistic way, to talk freely of the good and the bad while viewing the dead nostalgically and with understanding. This coming to grips with anger and guilt, this dealing with the reality of life, is part of the growth and change that grief can bring as the sufferer works out his or her ambivalent feelings. And now for the . . .

Success in Grief: Identification

Freud regarded identification with the deceased—literally taking the dead person psychologically into oneself (internalization)—as the ultimate task of mourning, the action that makes possible the cutting of the ties to the dead. Once the deceased becomes part of the bereaved there is no longer any need to rely on the dead person, for the loss has been made up in a sense, the hole left by the loss has now been filled and the bereaved is now able to talk freely and to think about the reality of the deceased with warmth and nostalgia, to recognize both the good and the bad.

Death is always described as a loss. The bereaved say they

have a hole left inside them, and to fill it at times they may take on the characteristics and even the mannerisms of the deceased. The survivors may carry out the wishes of the dead, even think like them. As this internalization goes on, the ties are actually being cut, the emptiness inside is filled and the work of mourning is thus successfully completed. The bereaved are now whole, free and able to invest all their feelings in another and rebuild a new life. It's not an easy concept to understand and takes a bit of thinking.

Another part of grief behavior that causes difficulty is . . .

The Regression That Takes Place

Any pressure on the human being—even a simple cold—causes him or her to regress, to act like a child, to seek the protection he or she once knew as an infant. Which is why you often hear, "When Joe or Mary or whomever has a cold, he or she acts like a baby." Actually we all want the protection of a parental figure, the mother, when we're sick or frightened. Grief is no different. Under these psychological pressures, all human beings desire to return to the comfort and protection of the womb. Yet most people feel ashamed when they find themselves behaving like small children in their fits of anger and irrationality during their bereavement.

A terrible mistake made in our culture is invariably to equate self-control with strength and maturity. Under pressure, strength really lies in accepting oneself and the very normality—the humanity, if you will—of behaving like a simple human being. Lily Pincus describes in her book how one tormented, bereaved woman wrapped herself in a soaking-hot bath towel, and curled up in her favorite chair in the fetal position. Help like this made it possible for this same woman then to go on and perform her part of her husband's memorial service.

By using this knowledge and their very human patterns, human beings can rise to the heights of their power to turn grief into growth, loss into gain. By expressing emotions one can learn to avoid the trap into which Victoria fell, for she never got over her violent anger at her son, the Prince of Wales, when her husband died. Instead of recognizing the normal irrationality and anger at bereavement, she blamed her husband's death on the fact that an escapade of her son's had led Prince Albert to travel to Cambridge to deal with their son's improper behavior. Albert returned ill from the trip and died from this sickness. Victoria never forgave the Prince of Wales: "It quite irritates me to see him in the room," she once explained. In Victoria we see the tragic effects of a failure to do the work of grief, to probe the feelings that come with grief, and that is what our next chapter is all about, the so-called pathological (literally "disordered in behavior") or inadequate grief.

CHAPTER FOUR

The Unfinished Business of Grief:
The Mourning That Never Ends

To every thing there is a season, and a
time to every purpose under the heaven:
A time to mourn, and a time to dance;

Ecclesiastes 3:1,4

When the work of mourning isn't done, when there is "unfinished business" left hanging, when the grief work isn't carried to completion, then the bereaved person is left with many problems to surface in a variety of ways and to affect his life seriously. Queen Victoria, for example, mourned her husband, Prince Albert, as long as she lived: ordered his clothes to be laid out each day after his death and water set out for his shaving; everything was kept as he had left it. In Eugene Field's poem "Little Boy Blue," the toys, too, are kept forever awaiting the little boy who had died. Many people are swept by overwhelming emotions of acute grief on certain anniversaries (the day of the deceased's death or birthday or wedding or whatever), no matter how many years pass. There are others whose health or whose marriages are seriously damaged by unresolved grief and some can no longer lead a normal life as a result of this mourning (or the lack of it). There are the parents and wives of soldiers missing in action who are stuck at the denial stage of grief and insist their loved ones are still alive (we see this today in some of the families of Vietnam veterans missing in action).

For such people there is no end to mourning, no turning to the dance nor resolution of their grief with the restitution of normal life and its share of happiness. For these mourners there is neither growth nor change, no recognition that the dead must be buried and a new life begun. There is no acceptance by these people of the fact that the bereaved must let go, must separate from the dead and recover from their mourning. Such people are what psychoanalysts speak of as "fixated," tied to this stage of mourning: they cannot move ahead with the resolution of their bereavement until they finally retrieve their emotional investment in the deceased so that they can then reinvest it in living people and in life itself.

The very terms that the experts (psychiatrists, psychologists and sociologists particularly interested in grief and mourning) apply to the various forms this type of grief takes clearly spell out the variety of problems involved: pathological, uncompleted, ineffective, complicated, inhibited, chronic, delayed, prolonged. The inability to experience good grief, the necessary mourning, can also lead to the so-called "anniversary reaction" which may strike without warning at a time far distant from the cause (this can be five or fifty years after the death, and in one instance we'll discuss later it was precisely nine nears from the very hour of death).

There are even early intimations of the problems ahead for certain mourners, warning signals in the patterns of early grieving or in the past of the person. The mourner's early life, the reactions in the first stages of grief, even the presence of the equivalent of Linus's blanket (taking its name from the "Peanuts" comic strip) are all signs to alert the knowledgeable observer to the need for professional help.

All too often it is the person who fulfills our national way of mourning, the one who is virtually or seemingly the all-American mourner who gets into trouble. These "strong" silent ones are far more likely to run into serious problems than the seemingly "weak" grievers, the ones who let it all hang out. Yet inadequate grieving occurs in nature also, as nature itself—for even among animals we see some of this disturbed kind of mourning.

It's not just the seemingly strange grieving but the very quiet, unexpressed kind that may end up as pathological mourning. But how then can one tell the warning signs? The answer to this question is a good deal of what this chapter is all about: the forms that inadequate mourning may take, what lays the groundwork for this and in whom and under what circumstances it is likely to appear. We will probe the manifestations and effects of these problems and what can be done for them. In short, here is the information for recognizing the problem—or even being aware of its appearance ahead of time—and where you can turn for help should it appear.

But first let's see how one can tell.

Grief: Telling the Good from the Bad

We've already seen what good grief with its pain and torment is, but only through it can the bereaved find the road to recovery. It's easy to see why people would like to avoid all this pain, and why some try to. But out of this good grief comes recovery, growth and change, the opportunity to cut the emotional ties that bind to the past, to bury the dead. All this is necessary so that one can go on into the future and build a new world which no longer holds the deceased, to form new relationships, since there is nothing that can be done to alter the tragic loss that has been suffered.

On the other hand, "bad" grief, if you will, is the inadequate or uncompleted mourning. Here the bereaved goes on living in the old emotional bondage which like all forms of peonage keeps its vassals in perpetual slavery. In bad grief one loses the opportunity to mature and change, is left to go through life permanently shackled to the long ago.

The basic difference is simple: uncompleted or inadequate grief is that mourning that leaves the survivor unable to cope properly with life. Emotionally disabled, these people are hampered and incapable of a satisfying existence. A widow, under the best of circumstances, may not be able to remarry because there are just too many widows and not enough unmarried men. But those widows who have failed to work out their grief will not be able to find new, satisfying roles for themselves in life. These inadequate mourners may not even be able to form new personal interrelationships, to get jobs in which they can function well and be happy, they may suffer a variety of physical ills, and so on.

Actually these problem mourners may go through perfectly normal patterns of mourning—but to an exaggerated degree—and they seem to stop or fixate at some level, to fail to move on, to mature. It's almost as if a child stopped growing at two or four or ten, physically or emotionally or socially or whatever. The result cannot be a happy life for the child who would then lose contact with the world around it. Everyone and everything would be maturing and becoming different while the child would become increasingly isolated and out of step. Such people live a sort of "stop the world, I want to get off" kind of existence, the people who live back in the past.

The Types of Inadequate Grieving

Essentially this is a matter of not enough mourning or a kind that isn't carried deep enough. When this happens there is no opportunity for the wound that is grief to be adequately aired so that it can heal properly instead of leaving a running sore, another permanent weak spot—a festering wound instead of a cleanly healed scar.

The problem itself of course always goes back much further than the immediate or current loss. As we've seen, the death of a loved one is really only a more permanent and therefore more traumatic separation than the previous earlier ones such as birth or leaving one's childhood or the teens or changing jobs. But the way each one reacts to a death is determined by the way the person has learned to deal with the many separations that occur in life; by the way he or she—as child or adolescent—saw the parents handling their separations and those events of life that each one has had to deal with (early loss of a parent, perhaps; immigration).

If these early separations and losses were handled by the parents in a strong, healthy manner, teaching how to use loss for growth and change, then the youngster will do the same as an adult, will experience not inadequate mourning but only good grief. As for the grief itself, the real difference between the good and the bad or inadequate is a matter of degree, of quantity and quality, not of the actual hurt or pain, the shock and the crying, the numbness and the rest, even in those who bury it all and never show grief.

The reactions in inadequate grief take a number of forms so that it's best to discuss these individually in view of their importance—understanding them will help those who must live with them as well as the families or friends who would like to help. The problem is inadequate or uncompleted or unresolved mourning, for if the grieving could be carried through to completion, there would be no problems. Here then are the basic forms these take.

Inhibited Mourning

This is the kind that shows up right at the start because these bereaved show no reaction initially, no grief on the death of the loved person. Typically these individuals fulfill the great American picture of the "strong" person, the one who exhibits no disturbance from the loss. This stoical or pioneer fortitude is unfortunately much admired in our society: children are admonished not to show feelings too openly, not to sorrow—"big boys (girls men, women) don't cry" is a common lesson that children absorb at their mothers' knees. To make matters worse, this is often tied to the similar and excessive repression and denial of anger as well.

Mourners are very well aware that others are made uncomfortable by any open expression of their feelings, for example by crying. Many men, at least in the past, have avoided firing women simply because they couldn't stand the tears. And weeping has long been used by women to gain their ends or avoid what they don't want. But in their coping with grief, this pattern has turned upon Americans. The mourner—conforming to the culture—feels "people don't want to see adults cry," and so the feelings are repressed and denied.

However, keeping feelings bottled up is a bit like heating a pressure cooker indefinitely—sooner or later the buildup has to find some release. Instead of blowing a safety valve, the person is likely to displace his or her feelings, and they then appear as physical or psychic reactions. Thus Lindemann feared that those who avoided the pain of good grief might instead develop such conditions as rheumatoid arthritis, ulcerative colitis, asthma or various emotional disturbances.

Inhibited mourners typically are the ones who hide behind the intense activity of practical arrangements, a frenzy of activity devoted to such jobs as arranging the funeral, cleaning up all details left by the bereaved or the last illness or whatever. There is a compulsive sort of "busyness," an involvement with a variety of ritualized activities the net result of which is to provide these problem mourners with defenses against their own feelings. These people become very busy with all the physical tasks and problems of the death but carefully avoid the very real emotional work of grief.

With no other means of expressing or ventilating the enormity of emotion involved in the death of a loved one, these people will turn to physical complaints such as Lindemann noted, and I have often seen tension headaches used to express the affect of grief, where the real pain was the anguish of bereavement. Sometimes it needs relatively little psychotherapeutic intervention to provide the needed help, and with this goes relief of the physical symptoms which may consist of an almost unlimited variety.

Inhibited grief can produce serious, destructive, long-range physical or emotional or family fallout. But one thing alone is certain: repressed mourning is going to produce damage whose form depends on the individual and his or her background which set the problem up, most likely in the early years of life.

But this of course is not the only problem, so let us now turn to . . .

Delayed Mourning

This may appear at first as inhibited mourning because there may be no early or initial grief, only to have the repressed or denied process explode in the individual's face at a later date. Here too there is a surface calmness during the early days or months of bereavement, a period filled with intense activity which may be betrayed by the haste with which things are done and the poor judgment frequently exercised during this period which itself is somehow filled—suspiciously so—with often contrived busyness.

Delayed mourners are particularly likely to suffer from the anniversary reactions we will discuss later. But such mourners are people who go through life like soldiers moving through a heavily mined field—they never know when some step will trigger a very damaging explosion. Delayed mourners may find their eventual flood of grieving triggered off by the birthday of the deceased, a wedding anniversary or the anniversary of the death itself—or the death of someone else may set off the grief reaction. Virtually anything may open the floodgates, and the longer the grieving is postponed, the more severe it will be when it finally comes.

In addition to carrying all the emotional problems of inhibited mourning, delayed grievers also find themselves turning to physicians for frequent help for their many physical complaints (a displacement of the pain of the loss). As in inhibited mourning, these physical problems can run the whole gamut of psychosomatic disorders. One widow suffered markedly from a skin condition, and when that cleared she began to complain of a burning on her tongue which eventually shifted to intestinal pain, and so on from one organ system complaint to another until psychiatric help finally cleared the real problem, the delayed mourning. In a sense, just the opposite is. . .

Prolonged or Chronic Mourning

This has also been called unlimited mourning and the terms themselves explain the problem—that of Queen Victoria with her lifelong mourning or Poe whose shadow will lift "Nevermore." Even in good grief the survivor will often want to do only those things the dead one would have liked, but this pattern goes on to resolution and everything is moved toward a normal life.

Victoria and the pattern of Little Boy Blue were quite typical of chronic mourning in that everything was kept the same as when the deceased was alive—chairs or toys or other objects. Some widows will even set the dinner table as if the dead spouse were still there or buy supplies for the deceased. Actually all this is a defense against grief, a denial that there has even been a loss.

While many observers feel it is quite normal for parents who lose a child to mourn the rest of their lives, this does not prevent a perfectly normal life, happiness in the family life, other children and relationships—but the pain and the sorrow of the bereavement remain strong, and they are readily aroused when memories are stirred by any appropriate time or object or place.

The Biological Aspects of Chronic Grief

Those who have had very much to do with dogs—or even read much about them—are aware of the effect the death of the master can have on the animal. Dr. George Pollock (one of America's leading experts on mourning and whom we've already met) tells the tale of two dogs. One was a fox terrier whose teenage mistress was killed in a school fire. Three times the dog ran away from the family home to sit in front of the school. Finally the mother locked the dog in their house, whereupon, mournfully, the dog crawled under the young girl's bed and for four days neither ate nor slept. When he finally improved he still waited at the house door in the afternoons, looking for his teenage mistress to come home.

And a Japanese dog called Hachi was owned in 1924 by a professor at Tokyo University. Hachi accompanied his master to the railroad station every day where he would await the professor's return in the afternoon. After little more than a year, the master died and the family moved to a distant part of the city. Nevertheless each morning Hachi would find his way to the railroad station and remain there until the evening, awaiting a master who never returned. Hachi performed this daily trip for ten years until he died. The Japanese put up a statue of the dog in front of the Tokyo station and in 1953 even issued a stamp in his honor.

Our human need to deny death is seen, too, in the behavior of apes, champanzees and baboons—and photographs in an issue of *Life* some years ago showed similar behavior on the part of elephants. Some animals even seem to have some of the acute grief reactions of man himself. Evidently this separation or loss reaction is buried deep in the human psyche, for it extends back down the evolutionary tree and must have been present long before man himself appeared.

But now let's look at a very special form of inadequate mourning.

Pathological Grief

This is a more precise condition than the more general and often intertwining forms of incomplete mourning which we have already discussed. Dr. Volkan, a world authority on this often bizarre condition and University of Virginia professor of psychiatry, has developed a specific and effective new therapy for this problem—what he calls "re-grief therapy." Pathological grief is—like the other forms of inadequate grief—the result of a failure in the normal mourning mechanism. Dr. Volkan has found that by taking the sufferer back in time to do the necessary regrieving, he or she can finally experience good grief with its healing values and its restitution, with its ability to free the mourner to grow and change.

As Dr. Volkan explains: "If you consider grief as a process, say a, b, c, d, e, then its complication may take place at any level, a or b or c, whatever, at the initial level or the denial one." The Virginia psychiatrist has found that virtually all his pathological grief patients have suffered sudden losses (either the result of a totally unexpected accident or even of a prolonged illness where the survivor had not prepared himself or herself for the coming loss) but experienced the death as a sudden, unanticipated one.

Dr. Volkan finds that pathologic grievers are very ambivalent people. The psychiatrist would consider the possibility of this condition if some six months or so after the death the survivor was only accepting the reality of the death intellectually while still denying it emotionally—desiring the return to life of the deceased while simultaneously fearing and even dreading it.

Typically, the pathological mourner will, for example, speak to the deceased in the present tense (say, "My father likes to hunt," or "My sister has blonde hair"). These mourners also dream of the deceased as seemingly engaged in a life-and-death struggle, with the dreamer attempting rescue only to be prevented by awakening. These mourners are often so "preoccupied with the dead person" that this interferes with their daily lives. One such person repeatedly moved the coffin from one place of burial to another for several years, since the mourner was constantly thinking about the deceased being unhappy in the current site of burial. Another mourner would run after people who passed on the street to see if it was the deceased.

What Dr. Volkan has come to term "linking objects" is a strange phenomenon that is also typical of these mourners, and actually connects to the birth of the human infant. Psychiatrists have found that it takes thirty-six months for an infant to feel and behave psychologically as if he or she were an individual in his or her own right and not merely an extension of the mother. To cope with this very early separation problem, the child turns to a so-called "transitional object"—the "security blanket" or "Linus's blanket." This is typically something soft and recognizable by its odor, such as a teddy bear or a pillow, and is held onto for solace, especially at bedtime. As Dr. Volkan explains laughingly: "The mother can't wash the darned thing or the kid won't accept it; it has to have a certain smell, a certain dirtiness to it." This is a normal stage of development, and the security blanket is discarded when it's no longer needed.

The psychiatrist finds a distinct similarity between the transitional object of the child and the linking object of the pathological mourner—both adopt and use these objects for the purpose of coping with a separation. However, the linking object is chosen from among the deceased's belongings (say, a watch or a camera); is perhaps a representation of the deceased (a photograph) or something that was at hand when the mourner either got news of the death or saw the dead body (perhaps a phonograph record being played at the time).

But these linking objects are not normal keepsakes, such as are retained and treasured and used (I have a red vest of my brother's, and as the pain is being replaced by nostalgia I enjoy wearing it).

But where most of us would keep and use a watch, the pathological mourner to whom this is a linking object would put it away, be sure always to know just where it is—but also be able to avoid it whenever desired to do so. The behavior exhibited toward these linking objects is often virtually grotesque—leaving a photo under a water leak or not washing an electric razor. This occurs because these mourners endow the linking objects with magical qualities, and the mourner uses them to express his feelings about either the dead person or the relationship.

The pathological mourner also characteristically shows an absence of the normal good grief and its symptoms. Or this person may also suffer—typically—chronic mourning with such normal symptoms of acute grief as crying or sighing, sleep disturbances or preoccupation with the deceased continuing for years. Often these mourners will have a delayed grief reaction although there may be hidden symptoms. With this delayed type, an anniversary may precipitate the open symptoms, as with one person who reacted exactly nine years to the hour and day after the parent's death. A teenager at the time of accidental death, this mourner had to take over all practical matters for the family and simply had no time for personal grieving. Now on this ninth anniversary, the survivor goes to the door—where news of the original fatal accident was delivered—and suddenly collapses, requiring medical care.

The regrieving that Dr. Volkan has developed for these patients consists of short-term therapy (often just a month or two) in which the pathological mourner in essence goes through the grief he or she never experienced. The patient now has the opportunity to experience the good grief that is so essential to the healing of the wound, to the restitution and recovery that is the aim of all healthy, normal grief.

In this way the individual can finally be freed to go on in his or her development into a whole new world. For usually pathological mourners have been fixated at the early childhood level of separation and individuation due to some traumatic experience. For example, the mother might have been hospitalized frequently and so separated from the child, or a parent might have died or left. The child might have been passed on to grandparents or adopted parents. Pathological grief is a good illustration of the intertwining roles of separation and loss and grief—and of their connection to growth.

We have also seen how often anniversaries can precipitate reactions, but sometimes these are problems of their own.

The Anniversary Reactions

Dr. George Pollock is particularly known for his studies on these strange phenomena in which a particular hour, a special day, a certain season, a specific anniversary or year may trigger severe and often violent responses. As Dr. Pollock puts it: "If there's an anniversary reaction, that's an indication that something's not right, not worked through. The presence of an anniversary reaction is an indication of uncompleted or abnormal mourning."

These reactions may even be strange occurrences which seemingly have no relation to the loss of a loved one five, ten or fifty years earlier. The reactions themselves may be emotional, making themselves felt in contributing to serious marital difficulties and even causing marriages to break up, bringing on anxieties and depressions, along with a host of assorted physical problems such as heart attacks, rheumatoid arthritis, hives, ulcerative colitis, migraine, hypertension or the familiar irritable colon syndrome.

Dr. Josephine R. Hilgard, Stanford University professor of psychiatry, tells how the artist Vincent van Gogh was born on the exact day and month one year after a brother who died before the great painter's birth. Both were listed in their parish register of births with the same number—29—and the painter eventually committed suicide at the age of thirty-seven on July *29.* This is the sort of thing one would expect with anniversary reactions where a day or date or whatever carries significant memories. Similarly Winston Churchill died on the anniversary of his own father's death (January 24).

As Dr. Pollock points out, this appearance of emotional or physical problems on particular times or days or holidays is simply that the times, the anniversaries, act as the trigger by which some repressed problem is released in the form of the anniversary reaction. But the question that cannot yet really be fully answered is. . .

Why Should Mourning Be Inadequate with Some People?

There are many elements which can turn the perfectly normal mechanisms of good grief into an inadequate or uncompleted form. Perhaps first we should review again the pattern of good grief. The first response is one of shock with its numbness and denial, its panic reaction with crying or wailing, even collapse. Then comes the acute grief reaction with its deep sorrow and pain, the sighs and restlessness or apathy, the searching and denial, the pining and the memories, the sleep disturbances and hallucinations and all the rest. And finally there is the third stage with its restitution and resolution, its healing and slow subsidence of the symptoms of grief with the gradual resumption of normal activities.

This initial response to death, the way human beings deal with the death of an important or loved person, depends on a variety of factors which will reveal what we know about the underlying causes of inadequate grief, uncompleted mourning or the various problem kinds. Dr. Volkan lists these as follows:

First is the type of death, whether it's been expected or whether it comes as a surprise. Pathological grievers usually give a history of unexpected or sudden deaths. The Harvard Study, as well as Dr. Parkes and others, also found that when a death is unexpected, there is a much greater likelihood of inadequate grief, of prolonged mourning or of such other problems as difficulties on the job, physical illnesses and so on.

Second is the mourner's rapport with the deceased. The more mature the relationship, the more likely the mourner will primarily feel a deep sadness, a personal and intimate affect with no guilt. However, when the relationship has been an ambivalent and stormy one, with a great deal of love and anger and hostility in it, then the mourner is likely to suffer a complicated or inadequate grief which may show itself in a number of ways. Many experts feel that strong ambivalences with their confused love-hate feelings are what produce much of the problems in mourning.

Third is the psychological makeup of the bereaved, and here the mourning is based on all the patterns of separation that the mourner has learned from birth. The more dependent the personality, the more likely, too, is inadequate grieving. There may also be "unfinished business" with the deceased—situations in which death has prevented the healing of wounds and conflicts, of anger and incidents (siblings who haven't talked for years, parents who haven't forgiven their offspring for marrying or living in a way they couldn't accept, extramarital affairs, or any of the myriad family difficulties that arise).

Fourth is the cause of death (illness, accident, suicide or some other form of violence). Any kind of violent death or suicide may produce severe affects and arouse, as Dr. Volkan puts it, "oppressive feelings of guilt."

And finally there are the very real problems of life. Death of the wage earner, for example, can lead to loss of home or status or the introduction of serious economic problems.

Can Lifelong Grief Ever Be Normal?

This is one of those debatable questions which are in part semantic—for prolonged grief is abnormal, yet lifelong grief may be normal. Many leading experts such as Drs. Pollock, Parkes and Gorer feel that the loss of a child (especially an adolescent or younger child) is not only a bereavement that has the longest-lasting affects, but that it is perfectly normal for the parents, and particularly the mother, to grieve permanently. However this kind does not interfere with life, even though the pain, the memories, the pining go on. One bereaved mother told me that even after nearly ten years the ache is still as deep and painful and sharp as ever, that she still sees her daughter as clearly as ever.

There are experts who find that widows, too, may mourn permanently for their husbands. As they put it, "I'll never forget him"—and this may be true. Right now, however, this must be left for further research which is very much needed in inadequate grief.

But there is one thing of importance to all those with one of these problems in mournings.

Where to Find Help for Inadequate Mourning

Normal grief, of course, needs no special help; it takes care of itself and with time the mourner heals and recovers. But when the bereaved suffers from inadequate mourning, then professional help is most often needed to make healing and recovery possible, to move the mourning off dead center and open the way for the necessary growth and change.

The two most widely available sources of help are the family doctor and the minister. Today, increasingly, both—and more particularly the ministers—are becoming aware of the emotional problems involved in the handling of grief and are having information and training made available to them through their respective professions and schools.

Perhaps these doctors and ministers are most valuable in their knowing when more expert help is needed. This specialized help can come from a psychiatrist or clinical psychologist, even psychiatric social workers. Many of these professionals are increasingly interested in grief and mourning—like Dr. Volkan or Dr. Pollock—and your minister or physician should know these people available in your community.

There are also groups of mourners and particularly the widowed who are banding together to help each other. But these groups are really not there to deal with the serious problems such as we have just discussed in this chapter. However, part III deals more fully with the kinds of help available and where to obtain it.

If the mourner can get no adequate reference from a physician or minister, often the name of someone capable in this area can be obtained by a call to the largest local medical school or hospital.

Now, however, we must look at certain grieving and funeral patterns of the past, the present and the future, and of the role of religion in bereavement. Finally we will even look at what some beliefs have to offer for the mourner today.

PART II
THE SPECIFIC PROBLEMS AND FORMS OF BEREAVEMENT

Religion, Afterlife, Burial, Cremation and Mourning Practices: The Help They Offer

> . . . for the Lord shall be thine everlasting light,
> and the days of thy mourning shall be ended.
>
> Isaiah 60:20

Man has always known that he is no more than a tiny ant trumpeting on a grain of sand in the universe. Lonely, naked, frightened, with all his vast technology, his atomic power and space flights, he is still tossed about at the whims of a Nature whose violence is far more powerful and destructive than man's most potent hydrogen bomb. So he has always lived, and still does, in terror of his world, quaking before its might and turning to witch doctor or physician or priest to shield himself from forces beyond his control. For man stands hesitantly before the twin forces of life and death, virtually as he did millions of years ago when he first wandered about on this planet.

Just as he did then, so man today still trembles, fearful and ignorant, before the unknown that is death. Fumblingly, he reaches out, striving to comprehend and to come to terms with whatever is out there where no man—neither astronaut nor scientist nor priest—can hope to go and return with the information needed to ease man's terror. Yet man does what no other animal can: he foresees his own end, has to face his own certain death and always live in its shadow. Not surprisingly, over the millenia there have been few who could, like Socrates, face their own death and calmly say that I go to die and you to live, and which of us has the happier outlook only God can tell.

Which is why mankind has turned to religion throughout his long history. For only in religion is there any hopeful explanation for what happens after death, a promise to relieve the terrible fear that man feels for the complete end to everything, the total separation from all the things that are so important to each of us—our loved ones, the world itself with all its beauty, the work we do, our possessions, everything else that makes life so precious and so worthwhile.

Many behavioral scientists theorize that it is man's overwhelming concern with death that has led to the development of religion. For death and its denial (in the form of immortality beliefs) have always been in the forefront of both man's thinking and his terrors. Man's total involvement and immersion in both life and death have made religion one of his first interests and greatest concerns. Right from the start, man turned to witch doctors and shamans, priests (or priestesses) and medicine men. Our earliest known painting (some twenty thousand years old) can still be seen in the caves of southern France—a picture of a medicine man in the skin of a bison. But man's concern with death goes back to Paleolithic days, perhaps as much as three hundred thousand years ago or more, for there were even then funeral and probably religious rites because Stone Age man, too, buried his dead and added food and tools for the needs of the deceased in the life after death.

Religion has always brought rituals with it and, in a sense, religion is ritual and myth. Unfortunately, religion admits of no scientific proof: no one has ever brought an apple back nor is anyone likely to do so from whatever is there in any afterworld—but then there can be no *dis*proof either. It is an orientation, a general feeling of otherworldliness. Religion calls for and offers a spiritual or otherworldly interpretation of life, and in this it gives something that none of man's other belief systems can. In religion the believer can find an explanation for both life and death, and virtually all religions promise some kind of life after death.

It is this concept of an afterlife, this rejection of death as the final and total separation, that characterizes religions and gives them a good deal of their hold over man during the millions of years that he has lived his death-haunted existence on this planet. From the psychiatric point of view, religion and its rituals also help to resolve the inner conflicts, the ambivalences, that plague man. In a sense, religions are set up by society to act as a defense that is consistent with reality, that fits into the real world of the believer and helps to cushion and protect him or her against the sort of psychic and cultural crisis that is death.

One anthropologist, Dr. Yehudi A. Cohen, has found that every known society believes that man has a spiritual life as well as a physical one. Cohen also believes that any afterlife is likely to be pictured pretty much the way the world of the believers is organized, socially or physically or both. Other anthropologists have also described the many and diverse belief systems and practices used by varied societies to explain death. These provide rituals which offer a form of cultural support for the expression or working out of the emotions of grief, in whole or in part. Where this is lacking, there are likely to be problems such as we will shortly discuss as we look at our own modern situation with its religions, its belief systems and rituals. But getting down to ourselves . . .

Religion and Afterlife in Our World

I'm a contributing editor of *Modern Maturity*, and only last year I did a series of interviews with the elder statesmen of our great religions and denominations: Catholic, Jewish, Protestant, Episcopal, Congregationalist, Unitarian, Quaker. The youngest of these clergymen was past sixty and had been in the ministry nearly forty years, so they spoke from long experience. They all agreed that there has been a drop in the numbers of those following their religion or denomination. That this drop in interest in religion is very widespread is emphasized by the fact that Gorer finds indications of decreasing belief in religion in Great Britain as well.

Nevertheless, belief in an afterlife, even in reincarnation, is something else again. Dr. Richard A. Kalish, a San Francisco behavioral scientist known for his investigations into death behavior, conducted a study recently on some 450 people divided equally among the ethnic groups in Los Angeles. As many as seven out of ten white Americans believed they would live on in some form after death while no fewer than four out of ten Mexican-Americans did so. Older people were more likely to believe in an existence after death than younger people—but there were *no* age differences in *wanting* an afterlife.

Mrs. Marjorie E. Mitchell, principal lecturer at a London college of education, reports that in December 1947 the British Institute of Public Opinion sampled Britons on whether they believed in a life after death and found that half said, "Yes," a third, "No," and the rest had no opinion. Less than half the men and more than half the women believed. Among various groups, nine out of ten spiritualists believed, slightly less than two-thirds of the Catholics, less than half of the members of the Church of England, and a third of the Jews.

And in the United States, Dr. George Gallup discovered in a 1966 poll that three-quarters of those queried believed that the soul does live after death. Dr. Glenn Vernon reports that an investigator questioning students in Midwest public colleges in 1964 found that over 81 percent of the women believed, as did two-thirds of the men. Obviously there is a deep basic desire in the human being to go on living after death—and the belief in an afterlife clearly must satisfy something in the great majority of human beings, at least in America.

Dr. Paul C. Rosenblatt, University of Minnesota behavioral

scientist, has put in, with his associates, several years on a broad cross-cultural study of death customs. In an analysis of seventy-eight societies around the globe—from Spanish Basques to Chinese peasants, from Copper Eskimo to Amazon jungle Jivaro—these scientists found an obvious consistency in the reactions to death, with the outstanding uniformity being in the emotionality of the reaction. So death is disturbing to all of us. And we all seem to have a need for some form of ceremonial dealing with the dead adults, for these investigators found it rare for this not to be done. Which points up the fact that there is more to the rites accorded the dead than the whims of modern man. Perhaps we should now look at . . .

Funerary Rites and Customs

We can learn much about grief and the rites and customs surrounding it by looking back to primitive man, for obviously if earliest man did things it was more likely to be on a basic human need basis than today's man does. The use of rituals and ceremonies in the process of disposing of the human dead is clearly as basic and universal as life and death themselves. The actual ritual processes were determined by a combination of the level of culture, the materials available (stone, copper, bronze and so on) and even the very climate (the hot aridity of Egypt lends itself, for example, to mummification), as well as the societal beliefs about an afterlife and the relationship the culture established between the dead and the living.

Here, too, the influence of the ambivalences we've seen so often in the reaction to death is felt. On the one hand there is the desire to retain the ties to the dead person while on the other and at the same time there is a wish to get rid of the deceased. There are fears of pollution and dread of the corpse, while in some rituals the bereaved will kiss the corpse or lie down on it. Some societies carefully mummify and retain the corpse while others break its bones or feed it to the sharks; some tie it hand and foot, bury it in all sorts of strange positions or simply burn it.

The corpse may be completely destroyed or totally preserved (as is done by mummification, say, with Tibetan holy men). Part may be kept—say the skull—or bits may be used as relics or may be worn as amulets (in the Andaman Islands). Food or tools, animals such as horses or dogs, servants, and even the wife may be buried with the corpse to provide for the trip to the afterworld or to make a better life there. Money may be buried with the body so that the dead can pay the boatman for ferrying him or her over to the land of the dead or to ensure the deceased will not be poor in that dim land.

The rites and customs of burial are as varied as man himself and his many societies, as different and ambivalent as the feelings about death (the anger and the love, the terror and the security, the hope and the guilt and all the rest). Which of these feelings becomes dominant often determines the handling of the corpse as much as the climate. But even on a single, small, Melanesian island, almost two dozen different disposal rites have been counted.

That it is all deep and basic, however, is clear. So strongly did prehistoric man work at making his burial arrangements permanent that our modern knowledge of prehistoric cultures in general has been made possible by the funerary arrangements of early man. For example, burial with personal ornaments such as amulets and figurines has been carried out since Middle Paleolithic (Stone Age) times, with their Cro-Magnon man, some three hundred thousand years or more ago.

Research carried out by Dr. Ralph Solecki, Columbia University professor of anthropology, in Iraq has revealed that Neanderthal man—some sixty thousand years ago—clearly had an advanced social and religious life. For it was obvious from the group of remains found that these primitive people cared for their lame and their crippled. One man who had a useless arm from birth even had had it amputated above the elbow early in his life and evidently had been cared for and protected, for he lived to a very old man (for a Neanderthal) of forty, what would be equivalent of about eighty to us today.

These burials were done carefully, with food provided and perhaps the remainders of funeral feasts as well. After a crypt had been scooped out among the rocks, the bodies were placed there and then covered with earth. The Neanderthals went to great pains with their burials, for microscopic studies made it clear that they must have searched the whole area to come up with the different species of flowers—bright-colored varieties in fact—that were buried with one particular male.

We tend to lose perspective today and this history helps to restore it. In the United States recently, interest in cremation has increased among Americans, a people who like to think everything done in their country is new, that anything that's old or obsolete is to be looked down upon. Yet cremation is actually both worldwide and prehistoric in origin. Destruction of corpses by fire goes back to the late Neolithic Period in Europe (perhaps some ten thousand years ago), and it began to displace burial (shades of modern America) during the Bronze Age, right on the heels of the Neolithic. Religions in which it was believed that the body was needed for resurrection—Judeo-Christian, ancient Chinese and Egyptian—then discarded this process.

But there was ambivalence about cremation even where it was accepted—in some societies it was used only for those of the highest ranks (leaders and chiefs), while in others it was used for the lowest, the criminals. The modern interest in cremation dates to the queen's surgeon in Britain, Sir Henry Thompson, whose book on the subject in 1874 virtually started it all in modern times, for he organized the Cremation Society of England. But the idea only took hold after World War II, and today about half the total bodies are cremated in Great Britain. In Australia and New Zealand there are more than a third, but in the United States, with almost four times the population of England, there are only about a third as many cremations performed.

But there may be good reason for moving back from this "modern" method—for good psychiatric reasons, for good grief. But to understand all this and grief, too, we must now turn to . . .

Funerals, Mourning, Immortality and Man

Death is a threat both to the person and to the community or society as a whole. As John Donne put it so well nearly four hundred years ago: "Never send to know for whom the bell tolls; it tolls for thee." We've already seen how death strikes at the individual, stirring up his or her fears and anxieties rooted in the very beginning of life, the concern with separation and loss. But for the community as a whole, death touches on other disturbing chords as well, both personally and socially, in that it destroys whole sets of complex interrelationships; disturbs established roles of authority, of economic and political and family status; shakes up the community as new leaders or chiefs or priests or hunters have to be replaced; confuses society's patterns as wives become widows and family units break up; threatens established values and institutions and patterns.

Not surprisingly, man has often been described as the "eternal protestant" against death and falls back on mechanisms of denial and repression to cope with the anger and the guilt and the myriad other feelings that arise at this time. But society, too, must fight back to reconstitute itself, to protect the individual from the storm of overwhelming emotions that follow this threat, this loss, this separation—to permit society itself to readjust successfully.

This protective response utilizes such mechanisms as funeral rites and customs, mourning and religious ceremonies and beliefs (especially that of an afterlife). After all, the disposal of the body is the simplest part of whole process, but it must be fitted into the rest of the pattern, must conform to the total system of beliefs so that it helps and does not clash with the rest. As a result, burial customs become far more complex than the simple disposal of the remains would necessitate.

This vastly complex system of beliefs and funerary rites and all the rest extends back to the very beginning of man, and in some of its elements (grief reactions for one), it even goes back into the animal world below man. As a result these response patterns are deeply rooted in the most primitive and ancient parts of man's own psyche. All this forms a basic design and a system that we interfere with at our peril.

Obviously the system has worked or it wouldn't have survived; it must have fulfilled the needs of both society and the individual. True, parts of it are window dressing and not essential, but even these usually reveal psychological, symbolic or mythical reasons behind them. Certainly the common eastern European practice of stopping all clocks, covering the mirrors and even the windows sometimes, has complex psychoanalytic reasons behind it, but too abstruse and debatable to make discussion here worthwhile.

Even today the whole complex system automatically goes into action at a death. Varying with the particular culture, there has been a certain general pattern followed in the United States during the past century. Family and friends are notified, ministers are called, and an undertaker. Yet until very recently, particularly in rural America, the women of the family or the neighbors joined in washing the corpse and clothing it, while the men built a simple pine coffin.

Today the funeral director (undertaker, or "doctor of grief" more recently) takes over this task, and embalming is commonly done in the United States (but rarely if ever in England). There may be viewing of the corpse, or simply a period between death and burial, whose length depends on the religion and may vary from virtually hours to days, or cremation may be utilized. Then there is the mourning that is determined by religion or society. And custom determines whether any special clothes (such as black) will be worn; whether there will be any other pattern followed (a meal after the burial, a variety of taboos, obituary notices in the local newspaper, involvement in social life, condolence calls and so on).

All this is an area of immense importance and considerable confusion today. When religion once set up rigid patterns, these were automatic procedures that protected the numb or confused mourner from having to make decisions at a time during which he or she is least able to think clearly and cope with such details. Religions even set the outside limits for mourning so that they brought the bereaved back into social involvement after a certain time had passed. And, finally, most religions carry a promise of an afterlife.

The Role of Funerals and Body Viewing

Perhaps the most serious and difficult problem the mourner faces is the need to accept the reality of death, to break through that typical, "I still can't believe it happened." The old-fashioned preparation of the body by family and friends obviously helped here, but many today say that the first awareness of the reality that "——— was really dead" came with the funeral.

The funeral serves also as a formal, socially recognized statement and recognition that this person has died, and as such it helps to bring home the reality of death both to the mourners and the community at large. It offers the first opportunity both for the individual and the group to start the long road toward restitution and readjustment—the first step on the way to good grief. Here, too, the ceremonies may provide a ritually controlled opportunity to begin the expression of the anger that goes with bereavement and even a lowering of the guilt and the anxiety.

Sometimes family members may kiss the loved one's cheek or lips, and the coldness of the body again brings home the fact that the person is dead. The Harvard Group has found that some widows like to put something from their marriage—a ring or pin or photo, perhaps—in the coffin, to be with their husbands forever. Actually this represents another attempt to refuse to accept the reality and finality of the death.

Many mourners, however, hardly remember anything from the funeral services simply because they are too numb at this point. I personally think much can be said for the Quaker-type services in which it is not a strange minister who barely knew the deceased but those who knew and loved the person well who speak, each out of his or her own deep feelings. I think it gives funeral services a very personal and meaningful content, both for those who speak and for those who listen. The personal involvement helps to break the denial as well.

Viewing the body is just another way of bringing home the reality of death, another way of breaking through the usual denial that the mourner has to deal with. Although half the Boston widows who participated in the Harvard Bereavement Study found the viewing of the body unpleasant, there are those who say that they couldn't believe their loved one was dead until they saw the body in the casket. Even seeing just the casket and knowing who is in it does help to bring home the terrible loss to all.

Even as I write this I can't help but say, "It's hard to believe," not only about my brother, but also about three friends whom I've lost over the last five or six years. That certain feeling of unreality does come back even after years, for what Dr. Volkan told me, "they will live in you," is true, and I can bring back memories of them—the way they looked or spoke—very readily and easily. So anything that helps to establish reality, to break down the powerful denial mechanism is valuable. Which raises the question . . .

What's Happened to the Burial?

As everything else about death, in late twentieth-century United States, burial practice has been cleaned up and sterilized, the religion and much of the reality taken out of death: the hard crying and the wailing, the deep feelings and the emotions, all are frowned upon. The old practices that brought family and community into close contact with each other and with reality are all gone: the body is now prepared by paid, uninvolved professionals; no more the muscular effort of lifting and carrying the coffin (then being a pallbearer meant something; now automation does it all); the grave is dug by machine; there are no violent expressions of powerful emotions at the graveside, no dirt on the hands from throwing in the soil to cover the coffin.

As Dr. Volkan tells of the funeral of a colleague: "I went to the funeral and at the graveside they left the casket standing above the ground and put it down only after everybody had left. That's not protection of the mourners when they don't let us see the fact that we bury somebody. We are protected *too* much from the process of letting someone go. We don't have much time given to the religious rites, so this whole business of getting rid of the dead people here is like getting rid of empty Coke bottles."

A Washington, D.C., psychiatrist put it to me: "These mourning rituals that have developed are important—reality tests, such as viewing the body, the burial service. But sometimes traditions are changed in ways that aren't particularly useful, like going out to the cemetery with the casket, setting it on the ground and then walking away. They do it universally now; they don't lower the body into the ground, so the experience of death and burial is that burial never occurs."

My own personal experience was similar, and I left the cemetery feeling somehow unsatisfied. I wanted to see the coffin (it was carefully covered and kept by the side of the hidden grave while a very few quick religious words were hurriedly spoken and then everybody marched away to the cars). When I discussed this with a physician, he remarked he had had exactly the same feelings when his wife had died and the cemetery services were the same as those I'd attended. I felt cheated out of the time to think and feel and contemplate while the coffin was lowered to its final resting place, to see it covered and the grave filled in, not to leave it to unfeeling strangers and machines to do mechanically and with no feelings or love.

A Southern psychiatrist pointed a finger of blame: "The ministers have abdicated. At one service the minister didn't even mention the young woman's name so that by the end one had forgotten we were there because of her. Religion can be a very personal thing, but this was a very sterilized ceremony." The funeral ceremony is important, or there wouldn't be these reactions to its shortcomings.

The whole funeral affair—the initial ceremony as well as the burial—has always been covered by a blanket of the supernatural. The rites have always been regarded as sacred or religious, matters for the whole society, the community at large, rather than simply a personal affair. So funeral processions get the right of way, cemeteries are protected by law even when set in the middle of great metropolises, and so on. It is rare, if ever, that a funeral service is conducted without some type of religious overtone, even though this may be a religion far different from the conventional. Thus the elements of the sacred and the supernatural are virtually always present, and they are usually accompanied by ritual.

Ritualized ceremonies, according to many behavioral scientists, serve to integrate the group and provide support. Memorial Day, for example, or Veterans Day are national funeral ceremonies which periodically help the United States to deal with death and perhaps even provide the nation with the oft-expressed concept of a triumph over death. Yet these ceremonies, too, always have a religious tone, an air of the sacred. So important is the role of religion in dealing with grief and death that Gorer feels we may have to invent ceremonies to take the place of those religious ones we have lost.

The role of cremation in bereavement, too, has been questioned. However, trained observers seem to feel that whether there is burial or cremation doesn't matter so much as whether there is a recognized ceremony or ritual involved to signify that there has been a death and to assist the mourners in working out their grief, to provide a supportive structure at this time when the bereaved need it so badly.

Dr. Parkes found that some widows, who were not prepared for the reality of death being brought home as powerfully as it is in the cremation process, reported feeling the horror of the experience, of seeing the coffin going into the furnace and being unable to forget it afterward. On the other hand, there seems to be an increasing move toward less services and simple disposition of the ashes without burial in the United States, thus taking all reality and ritual out of cremation. Parkes, interestingly, did find that the cremation, chosen for their deceased husbands by more than half the widows in his London study, proved more often disturbing than the traditional burial. Looking back at cremations in man's early history, it is clear that these were done with the same ritual and ceremony as were burials, emphasizing their importance, rather than the biological and sanitary need to dispose of the body safely, in the psychological help offered the bereaved which a traditional burial provides.

But now we must ask . . .

Where Does the Mourning Process Fit In?

There are two basic approaches to the meaning and value of the mourning process. One theory was developed by the famous anthropologist, Bronislaw Malinowski. This maintains that death rites and customs really provide a means whereby the society as a whole can readjust to the loss and release its emotions and tensions (the violent, ambivalent emotions such as anger and love, hate and guilt, the desire to maintain ties and to sever them, the terror of loss and separation). This was an essentially psychological approach.

But on the other hand, the famous sociologist Emile Durkheim maintained that mourning behavior (the weeping and wailing, the self-injuries, and so on) may be out of proportion to the actual strength of the particular emotions. Durkheim believed that this whole process really is not to release emotions and tensions but to create and express them and thus to strengthen and affirm the basic values of society, as well as its solidarity and morale. For example, the widow's weeping and crying are not to provide comfort for her but to assert publicly the importance and value of marriage.

Regardless of which side we take, there are still the very personal reactions of the mourner, the suffering and agony each one must go through. Regardless of the exact role that death and the mourning ceremonies play for society as a whole, death and grief are needed for each mourner individually to do the necessary work of mourning and develop his or her own maturation and alterations. The rites and customs that have grown up over hundreds of thousands of years—even millions perhaps—do help and protect the individual and we ignore them at our own peril.

Gorer is disturbed by the decline in the ritual observances of mourning and feels this lack (of religion, if you will) is at the root of a great deal of mental ill health among the bereaved. Parkes, too, has seen evidence that those mourners who fail to ventilate their anguish within the first week or two are more likely to be disturbed at a later date.

But this is the aim of the customs, rites and behaviors of mourning—to give the individual as well as his or her society the opportunity to express the feelings, the pain and the torment and the agony, the fears and the anger and love, all those ambivalent and confused emotions we have discussed in detail earlier in the book. Ideally, this mourning period with its rites and customs will give the bereaved an opportunity for socially approved expressions of their grief: open crying and wailing, withdrawal into self, even the regression that goes with loss and separation.

All that goes on during the mourning period, the funeral and the viewing of the body, the condolences and newspaper notices, even the people who visit and speak of the deceased in the past tense—helps to break through the denial of death, leads to the full realization and acceptance of the fact of death. The conventions and the social rites also provide the mourner with information as to the way he or she should dress and even function. And what is so very important, the customs also provide the mourner with some information as to when the mourning period itself should come to an end.

During this period, the wisdom of many tens of thousands of years becomes clear, for the rites that have been developed within religions, the wake of the Christians and the shiva of the Jews, demonstrate their value. Repeatedly, behavioral scientists I interviewed confirmed or said in their own words what has disturbed Gorer—that the decline in our adherence to the formal religions with their beliefs and customs and rituals has left man exposed to all those irrational and unpredictable storms of grief by taking away his long-developed and ancient protections, this important means of guidance which we call religion. But there is nothing to prevent modern man from deliberately developing new customs and rituals to fulfill the tasks of the old, to provide the same support and protection in a modern and perhaps more acceptable guise. But before we embark on such an ambitious task, we must understand the way these old forms work, and we might look at the oldest and best organized of these first.

The shiva and the traditional Jewish period of mourning closely corresponds, as Dr. Pollock explains, to the intrapsychic mourning stages and fits into the psychoanalytic understandings of grief. The ancient Jews utilized shrewd observation and a natural psychological understanding combined and refined over thousands of years.

Orthodox Jewish mourners are expected to be free of all obligations and not even comforted before the body has been buried. Then the first three days after burial are given up to weeping and lamentation: the mourner doesn't respond to greetings and visits are discouraged. During the seven days following the burial (which includes the first three), the mourner remains at home, can be visited and comforted, but wears a torn ("rent") garment, and, if a man, doesn't shave or groom himself. The torn clothing corresponds to the self-mutilation that was part of many primitive mourning rituals and seems a refinement serving the same deeply felt purpose of expressing the anger so widely felt at this time.

Then there is a thirty-day period (sheloshim) during which mourners are encouraged to gradually leave the house more and more so as finally to rejoin society and take their place in the community again. Then comes a twelve-month period during which full participation in society—with limited entertainment or amusement—goes on. After that, only on the anniversary of the death or at special holy days are certain ceremonies carried out for the dead: saying special prayers and lighting a memorial candle, for example.

If we look objectively at all this, it suddenly falls into place—the first period is clearly that of the initial shock, the numbness, that first claims the mourner. When the bereaved returns from the burial, there is a mourner's meal—this is not a celebration but an attempt to demonstrate that the mourner's life and relationships must now be resumed. Through this first week, the regressive needs of the mourner are satisfied as friends and relatives gather to take over all the necessary household tasks, to bring in the food and prepare it. They may even actually feed the principal mourner like a baby, thus recognizing the regression to the first separation individuation, the first thirty-six months of life.

The presence of those who care for the bereaved also provide relief from the mourner's feelings of loneliness, loss and isolation which arise at this time. Talking of the deceased also helps to bring recognition of the death, to end the denial that is so universal, to make it more possible and even comfortable for the bereaved to begin to talk and think of the deceased in such a way that the new relationship can be clarified and adopted.

This talking also permits—in the protection of the home and the presence of familiar, friendly and accepting people—an opportunity to ventilate all the feelings of grief, to express the pain and anguish, to cry and wail, to work out the guilt and perhaps some of the anger as well. The year of mourning actually corresponds roughly to what we know scientifically of how long it takes for the individual to begin successfully the resolution of his grief, the readjustment and restitution that will finally signal the end of good grief.

The wake, too, carries healing qualities with it, for it attempts to accomplish the same things as the shiva, although it is usually only three days. Virtually half the Boston widows in the Harvard Study found wakes helpful, and only a small handful thought them mostly negative. The wake—waking or watching—is actually an ancient custom going back long before Christianity itself. In this, a group of relatives or friends was invited to sit and commune with, say, a dead man in order to make easier his separation from the world he knew and to strengthen him for his entrance into the unfamiliar afterworld he was now entering for the first time.

When Christianity entered the picture, prayers were added to the vigil. The corpse, with a plate of salt on its chest, was slipped under a table on which alcoholic drinks were placed for those conducting the vigil. The drinks soon turned the "waking" into outright drinking parties. Then the Reformation came along and prayers for the dead fell into disuse, at which time waking, too, became obsolete in Great Britain. It still survives among Roman Catholics in the English-speaking world, particularly in Ireland, and can actually be found in many different cultures. Like the shiva, waking offers a variety of aids to the bereaved and fulfills virtually the same functions as the Jewish custom.

Both these patterns are there to permit public expression of grief and satisfy the regressive tendencies of this period. But all too often wakes and mourning rites today fail in their appointed tasks—as the Harvard Study has found—and simply become another occasion for the strict control of feelings. It would seem that only where the ceremonials are closely tied to the religion, as with shiva, are they successful today in their appointed tasks, for Americans and seemingly for the British at any rate.

In a sense, however, we are talking here of the rituals of religion as much as anything else. For folkways, too, can accomplish this same very considerable help. Dr. Volkan remembers, for example, when he was a young boy in Cyprus: during a funeral the women would lean out of their windows and scream angrily, "Why are you leaving us?" As he explains: "You see this element of anger, of not denying, of togetherness—the whole neighborhood crying and shouting . . . something's been torn apart from them and this is an appropriate emotional response, what you call grief." And then he added a remark that sums up the healthy way to handle grief: "It is not a shameful thing to grieve!"

But there is one question that often arises.

Where Do Religion and the Afterlife Fit In?

Man, it has often been said, is incurably religious, and certainly religion has been present as long as man himself, and as long as death and life. Religion and death are inextricably intertwined, and the religious approach to death virtually ensures the consideration of an afterlife.

There are many explanations given for the development of religion, but a very common one is that man's confusion about death, coupled with his sheer terror of it, have led him to seek an answer. Just like his modern descendants, primitive man, too, wanted to deny death, to have some promise of immortality. To find an explanation of death, man devised what we call religion, and then to conquer or at least to be able to live with his fear of death, he developed the concept we call immortality, a life after death. Out of all this the varied and complex belief system we term religion finally evolved.

All cultures devised rites and ceremonies and beliefs to deal with death, to control the individual's anxiety about his or her own eventual demise, and to soften the impact of this loss on the society as a whole. And when that society was small, say a tribe or a village, the loss of a member in his or her prime (and most did die in their youth until almost the twentieth century) was a serious blow to the existence and viability of the group. The device used to soften this shock was the belief in an afterlife, some sort of spirit existence after death, so that man need not face the cold, stark totality of his own end and the disappearance of himself as an individual and as a psyche when he dies. And so all cultures developed some sort of belief in an afterlife. Since it was to these spirits that man first turned for help, the first religion was an ancestor belief system and the first rites were funeral rites.

Yet despite all of this, we have seen a waning of religious belief in our time, but not of belief in an afterlife as we have seen from the figures cited earlier. Simultaneously, too, with this seeming drop in religious belief, there is an overwhelming rush toward the occult so that it would seem people today are simply exchanging one belief system for another—but preserving their belief in an afterlife. After all, modern man is just as fearful of death as his primitive ancestors.

And on the scientific level, Dr. Ernest Becker, the Pulitzer Prize-winning anthropologist, was quite clear in his *Denial of Death* when he called for the recognition of our struggle against death as being at the very core of all human existence, and the need for a totally new cooperative scientific-religious approach to life.

I found, as most people have, that those who deeply believe in religion and an afterlife seem to find more comfort in the face of the death of their loved ones. But what bothered me was simply whether this belief exacted a price, affected those who wanted to believe in a literal physical existence in some other dimension, some heaven or whatever. The question was an obvious one, and you may be interested in the answers from the supposedly antireligious world of the psychiatrist.

Dr. Peter Hartocollis, director of the C. F. Menninger Memorial Hospital (the world-famous psychiatric hospital of the Menninger Clinic) in Topeka, Kansas, answered my question as to whether belief in an afterlife was a healthy way to handle grief: "Yes, I would say so. . . . It's a sense of anticipation that may have a little bit of anxiety in it. It has a lot to do with what Erik H. Erikson (one of the world's leading psychoanalysts) calls the basic trust, the feeling of confidence that an infant develops with an adequate mother. You always have the anticipation of seeing the person who is not there. . . . This anticipation is a very pleasant one. It doesn't create problems; it's safe."

And Dr. Varmik Volkan put his thoughts on the role of religion this way: "Ceremonies definitely do help—yours would be different from mine, religionwise. They are something by which you notarize, so to speak, that the death occurred, for ceremonies are in the service of breaking down our denial. If you have ceremony, you do not deny the death as much as if you don't have one."

Dr. Castelnuovo-Tedesco sees it this way: "The comfort of religion occurs to fewer people today than at one time. Death would mean for many people not total annihilation but simply passing on to another world where one would hope to meet one's spouse, beloved parents, friends, relatives, people whose company one had enjoyed . . . whereas today most of us—or at least those who do not believe in an afterworld or share a particular religious belief—have to accept this very disturbing idea of passing on into nothingness.''

And when I brought up a particularly famous faith healer who sees an afterworld in which each of us will meet our loved ones in virtually a physical sense, the Vanderbilt psychiatrist went on: ''One would believe this is a source of strength and support to feel she can in some future time and place reunite herself, that she herself will not be utterly annihilated and banished into nothingness . . . that she will maintain some kind of recognizable identity by which her spouse will be able to recognize her.''

I was personally surprised to find these as well as others I queried were almost uniform in their recognition of the values of belief in an afterlife—so much so that it became pointless to quote the others such as Dr. George Pollock who called attention to the values of religious rituals in helping the individual achieve the adaptations of the mourning process. But you may feel quite differently—and the psychiatrists did not commit themselves to their own personal feelings and beliefs.

So now let us turn to the timetable of grief instead of its manifestations.

CHAPTER SIX

The Time Frame and Determinants of Grief, Who Suffer the Most and the Anticipatory Side: How Long It All Should and Does Last

> ¨To every thing there is a season, and a
> time to every purpose under the heaven:
> a time of war, and a time of peace.¨
>
> Ecclesiastes 3:1,8

While there is no precise hour-by-hour timetable for grief, there is a general time frame, broad limits within which the mourning process is worked out. Thus sometimes we can speak in terms of days, perhaps a week or so, while in others, years or even a lifetime is involved. Only when some of such time periods are seriously overstepped or entirely missed, can we be sure there is a problem, that danger signals are flying and help is needed. We also know something today of the factors that decide the path the bereaved must travel, which people with what sort of background or personality are likely to have trouble. We have some awareness, too, of who will feel grief the most and under what circumstances, and of the effect of the anticipation of the death of a loved one.

By knowing all of this, we can know when to seek help or advise someone for whom we care that professional aid should be sought. And while the child or the adolescent may not hurt the most, they are the ones who can be damaged the most. Losing a parent can even be fatal to a child (we will discuss their grieving problems fully in the next chapter). But for now let us look at adults and . . .

The Timetable That Grief Follows

The first days or even the first week following the loss of a loved one is a period of shock during which numbness clouds and softens the whole experience. This is a time of denial and disbelief, a period filled with weeping and wailing, of sighing and agitation such as we have already described. It's a period whose length is acknowledged both in shiva and the wake. But when this shock period extends beyond a week or so (except perhaps under particularly traumatic circumstances and even then experts would look closely at a longer time), it offers the first warning that something is going wrong with the usual normal grieving process.

The real pain starts as the shock wears off, and then there is the second period, the one of acute grief, which is filled with memories and preoccupation with thoughts of the deceased; with sadness and longing, searching and restlessness, crying and sleep disturbances; with loss of appetite and of interest in things in general. This second period usually peaks between the second and fourth weeks after the death, and begins to ease up after three months or so. But this acute stage doesn't really begin to come under control for as much as six months or so following the loss.

Finally, the third stage—that of restitution and resolution, of resumption of normal activities—takes over. In this, the symptoms so evident in the second stage begin to soften, to blur and to fade. Distress turns to sadness; remembrance increasingly becomes tinged with pleasant thoughts and memories; nostalgia enters where formerly there was only pain. This was previously thought to last no more than a year, the time span allotted in shiva, and in many other social and folk or religious customs.

But the Harvard Bereavement Study, along with other investigations, indicates that this grieving may actually go on for two or three years under normal circumstances, where a spouse, at least, is concerned. And investigators at the Harvard Laboratory of

Community Psychiatry, from which the Bereavement Study came as a research project, now seem to feel that most widows carry on the work of mourning for their lost husbands not for one or two or three years but for as long as they live. Gradually, however, the acute pain and responses soften, energies are restored, and the mourner moves back into the mainstream of life once more. The Harvard Group also found that it was more common for widows to begin seeing some rays of hope for their future during the second year following their loss rather than the first.

All mourners, observers agree, suffer marked grief reactions on the first anniversaries of any kind. Even many years later the survivor is likely to react to special times or objects. Thus the anniversary of the death, a photo or book of the deceased, a birthday or a marriage anniversary, and so on may produce feelings of sadness or even mild grief. But as the years pass, these responses become more transitory and affect the life of the survivor less. In fact this is probably the test of successful grieving, that after a year or two the bereaved is successfully functioning fully without serious interference from the grief.

However, the loss of a child—particularly a young one or an adolescent, even a young adult—is peculiarly traumatic and will certainly take longer getting over than that of a spouse. Those who have investigated these problems as well as those who treated such patients are in pretty general agreement that the loss of a child produces permanent grief, that it is never really worked through, particularly where the mother is concerned.

Dr. Marris, for example, found in his studies of London widows that they seemed to take about two years to recover from grief even though the acute symptoms usually only lasted a year or so. He also queried widows who felt the change that had taken place in them had been permanent and in this sense they really never got over the loss. But even this can be used for insight into the individual, turn loss into gain, as we shall discuss in our last chapter.

Further indications seem to confirm the long-lasting nature of widowhood, for Dr. Arthur H. Schmale, a University of Rochester professor of psychiatry and medicine, found that only three out of fourteen widows who had lost their husbands through cancer had worked through their loss and gone on to new interests, relationships and activities. And even after thirteen months of bereavement, Maddison found that more than a fifth of Boston widows and a third of those in Sydney, Australia, suffered a marked health deterioration.

In general, however, most mourners are at least started on the road to recovery with their energies restored after a year or so even though their grief may run on for considerably more time. But what of the intensity of this grief?

The Degree of Despair—and the Way It's Expressed

Dr. Parkes has broken much new ground in the problems of grief and bereavement, and his London study is now a classic. He studied twenty-two widows under the age of sixty-five and found they fell into three groups in their handling of grief, and in a sense they either benefited from or paid for the way they dealt with and expressed their emotions.

The first group of widows was very upset the week after their loss and continued so for the first and most of the second month, but by the time the third month rolled around, these women were only mildly disturbed.

The second group was only moderately upset during that first week, but most turned severely disturbed the second week. However, their grief soon disappeared, and then they recovered more quickly than any of the others.

But the rest of the widows displayed little or no affects during the first week, but by the fourth week they were all moderately or severely disturbed, and more so than any of the others. These women couldn't get away without showing emotions; they could only put them off. Even the first month saw these widows with more physical symptoms than those who let it all hang out, and thirteen months later this group who denied or repressed their emotions had their overall outcome rated "good" in only a single instance, while all the rest of their group had emotional symptoms of one type or another.

This last group included women who averaged some nine years younger and whose spouses tended to have suffered sudden death. They were "at risk"—the sort of person whose setup makes him or her more likely to have problems with grief, as we shall see a little later in this chapter.

Dr. John J. Schwab, University of Louisville professor of psychiatry, headed a team which did a study of bereavement in forty-five representative mourners in Alachua County, Florida, in 1970. His team found that half the mourners had an intense response to the death, one-sixth had moderate reactions, while slightly more than a third had a minimal response. Spouses and parents were most likely to have a severe reaction—race, sex and age had nothing to do with the level of grief. But more than a year after their bereavement, half of the interviewees still showed acute grief reactions.

There is, however, one thing that the bereaved quickly learn.

The Bad Times for Grief

The bereaved soon recognize that there are certain "bad times" as many of them put it. These are the times of day or week or month—or year—when the mourner finds he or she suffers the most distress. At first these occasions creep up on the unsuspecting and unprepared mourner. But the times the bereaved is taken unawares decrease, while simultaneously the affect of such incidents is diminishing in its punch, which during the very early days or weeks of mourning can come as a shattering blow, one which leaves the bereaved in tears or at best so disturbed that he or she may be left quite incapable of carrying on work or whatever for some time.

The bad times are those times of the day that carry a particular connotation, some special connection with the deceased. However, it is on awakening and at bedtime that mourners seem to hurt the most. I found the mornings hardest—to face the bleak gray day, to have to be aware that this day, too, would be empty, to know once more that my brother was dead. And somehow at nighttime I found it hard to go to bed, perhaps in part because I dreaded the dream and didn't want to go to bed until I was so tired I could go right to sleep. But even though at the time of this writing it is only six months past, I already find myself looking back at those times as part of my past except for the certain occasions.

The special occasions that can be bad, when the grief feelings come flooding back, are those like Christmas, New Year's, the deceased's birthday, perhaps spring or the first snow. These are the times that hurt when they roll around during the first year—and I found the sixth-month anniversary disturbing. Mourners I have interviewed have told me the same things in their own words and with their own personal variations—except for the mornings and the bedtimes which are bad, it would seem, for all the bereaved until the work of grief has been completed.

Widows will have a hard time when five or six o'clock comes on weekdays because this is usually when their husbands were expected home, and so they automatically start listening for the doorbell or the key in the lock. One widow I know feels it hardest during the day because she shared a joint profession with her husband and they had worked together in the same office which she still occupies. The evenings carry their own problems for widows and widowers because of the emptiness and the loneliness

One widower I know always eats out and avoids going home until he's so tired he can just flop into bed and go right to sleep.

If the deceased was a school-age child, then three or four o'clock will be the bad time—when the youngster came home from school. Mealtimes are painful for all mourners who lived with the deceased (spouses, parents of young children, the children themselves), for at this time the empty place at the table is a glaring, aching emptiness both inside and outside, so it's not surprising that denial can take the form of setting that extra place as if the missing one were alive.

Weekends and holidays are bad times for families because these almost invariably meant family activities, and the loved one is missed more acutely then. Family holidays hurt, too: Thanksgiving and Fourth of July, Christmas and New Year's, certain religious holidays, the opening of the baseball season to some, hunting season to others, ice-skating time, anytime when regular things were done together. Only the passage of time and the grief work can help, and sometimes this only makes the pain duller and easier to bear, a temporary, passing ache or sorrow. But time does, under the worst of circumstances—the loss of a child, say—make the grief such that it no longer interferes with life and functioning. And under many other circumstances (the loss of my brother, for example), time will allow nostalgia and a passing sorrow to replace the pain.

The test of good grief—of adequately working through the emotional problems of mourning and grief, of accepting the death and looking honestly at all the feelings that go with it—is that the mourner finally tolerates these bad times with passing pain or only slight, faint, sorrowful thoughts. The ideal is for nostalgia and pleasant thoughts, an ability to talk about the deceased with honesty and affection, finally to take the place of the aching pain and the grief and the distress.

But there is a special kind of grief that must be borne in mind since it affects many of us and is significant in the way we go on to do the work of mourning, and it must be reckoned with in our everyday lives since retirement and age produce their own grief.

The Promise of Anticipatory Grief

Anticipatory grief is like a full-dress theater rehearsal, a dry run, of what is expected. But those who rehearse a play or test military hardware look forward to success and survival, while those going through anticipatory grief can only look forward to loss or even death. Yet, anticipatory grief, when understood, recognized and handled jointly by both the future survivor and the dying, can give this limited period a quality many regard as unequaled in ordinary, everyday life.

The term "anticipatory grief" was first used by Lindemann who was thinking of the reactions of the families of soldiers and other fighting personnel who faced possible death in combat. Today, however, this term is applied specifically to the situation in which both the future survivor and the dying person are faced with an inevitable death, most commonly from terminal cancer. While the two face a different outcome (as Socrates said, you to live and I to die), both face the loss of love objects: for the dying person, the loss of everything, even himself or herself as an individual; for the survivor, the loss of a loved one.

With a mutual awareness of the problem, the two can work together—survivor and dying person—to make something good out of it all, truly to find gain in the loss. And this is why so many observers now urge that the patient be told the truth about the condition and the diagnosis and the future, because otherwise both the dying and the survivor-to-be are cheated out of those last days or weeks or even years which can be valuable, rich times.

Frequently under these circumstances family angers and clashes are put aside, and literally under the shadow of death, all things change to become richer and gentler and more loving. Estranged mates and relatives have rejoined, long-standing breaches have been healed, angers put away—as one dying cancer victim said: "Well, at least my cancer brought the family back together again."

This period, too, gives the survivors an opportunity to make amends for those many problems that produce anger and clashes within all families, perhaps by doing something the dying person wants or giving support and love at the time the human being needs these the most. Helpful as this period is to the dying, it can be even more valuable to the survivor who can look back on his or her own loving help rather than angry clashes, and so have that many less guilt feelings to be dealt with during bereavement.

The closeness and richness and love in relationships under the shadow of anticipatory grief have sustained many mourners and made their losses that much more bearable. This period has given rich memories and left wonderful times to be recalled when the pain and distress of the acute grief have subsided. It is also a time when the grief work is begun and so one might well ask about . . .

The Role of Anticipatory Grief in the Time Frame and Pattern of Mourning

In his classic article, Lindemann tells of the soldier who returned from combat to find that his wife no longer loved him but wanted a divorce—because of anticipatory grief. The Harvard psychiatrist felt the wife had worked through the anticipatory grief (felt when her husband was likely to die) so well that all ties had been cut! This same way of dealing with separation and loss has also led to frequent situations in which those released from jail or hospitals, as well as from military service, could no longer find any place left for them in their families.

This form of grief moves in what would seem odd ways at times. One would expect this mourning to get worse as the time of death draws closer. But it may not do so if this grieving has gone on for a particularly long time, and it can produce some unique problems.

For example, just as ambivalences are likely to lead to difficulties in mourning, they will do so—differently but perhaps more damaging—in anticipatory grief. For one thing, there are almost invariably decisions to be made—should a new physician be tried or another hospital, a different mode of treatment or a new experimental one? And with all this there are the overhanging feelings of anger or death wishes, conscious or unconscious, toward the dying person, the "I wish it were all over, I can't take it any longer" sort.

How many are there who, seeing a loved one suffering, didn't wish it were over, not only for the dying person, but also for themselves as well? This can be both for emotional and for financial reasons, even from simply being torn apart between the demands and needs of, say, the children versus those of a dying husband or other child, or even one's job. All this comes at a particularly difficult time, one in which the object of these feelings is peculiarly vulnerable, is fighting a losing battle for life anyhow, and so death wishes would likely seem even more powerful and threatening than ordinarily. Moreover, during this period the survivor is living through the death of the loved one in fantasy, again and again.

So anticipatory grief, like all the forms of grief, is ambivalent itself: while on the one hand it prepares the survivor for the event and does at least some of the grief work beforehand, on the other hand it also leads to guilt feelings which may interfere with the working-through process both before and after the death. The effects of this grief—like all of mourning—are dependent on the bereaved's past, what he or she has learned about separation and loss since birth.

The actual symptoms of anticipatory grief are those of ordinary acute grief with minor variations. But it is just because the person does go through these that some of the later work of mourning may be accomplished at this time.

However there is one pattern that has emerged that is unique to this period—what Dr. Glen W. Davidson, Southern Illinois University chief of thanatology, calls "The Waiting Vulture Syndrome." This shows itself in the drooping head, falling shoulders and general exhaustion of the despondent survivors-to-be who have accepted the oncoming death of a loved one and feel both helpless and guilty about being ready too soon. Thus physically they assume the characteristics of the waiting vulture. This situation resulted in a severe explosion in one family that had prepared itself when told the end was close—only to have the cancer victim rally suddenly and even talk of going home.

This is a particularly treacherous situation in cancer patients, since so often these estimates are quite far off. In a study of these estimates, Parkes found that nearly half (44 percent) of the estimates proved to be more than twice the actual length of survival, while 9 percent of the estimates proved to be less than half the actual survival time. In one instance I know of, the family was told it was a matter of only distant concern, whereas the illness proved to be fatal in about four months, so that there was false optimism and severe letdown. I experienced a very similar thing. It's best for all such estimates to be accepted with a very large grain of salt as a protection for the survivors-to-be.

The Waiting Vulture Syndrome is most damaging because the pressure on family is severe and bound to result in guilt feelings which can only be dealt with through knowledge. The family members must recognize that their reactions are perfectly normal: exhaustion, waiting for the end (the vulture feeling) and the wishes it were all over. There must also be the ability to recognize that these death wishes carry no power with them—the dying person will not be affected by them in the least. Understanding such a seemingly simple thing is the only way human beings can deal with this belief in one's own magical power, the influence of a wish, a pattern that goes back in human beings to earliest childhood and that creates problems in the loss of parents when young children are involved, as we will see in the next chapter.

But what of the opposite type of death?

The Anticipated Versus the Sudden Death

These two experiences—the anticipated loss and the one that strikes without warning—are vastly different in their affects even in the same group of mourners. The Harvard Study of younger widows and widowers (those whose spouses were forty-five or younger) showed clearly that there was a vast difference in the end result, the eventual recovery and restitution, when the mourner had a chance to work through some of the grief beforehand. There seemed little difference in the depth of the initial grieving between the two groups. Other studies (by Clayton and others), too, showed little difference over the first year.

However, it was in the eventual outcome that the big differences appear. The Boston Study found that, among both widows and widowers, the chances for returning to full functioning and finding happiness are distinctly better for those who went through anticipatory grief than for those who were plunged into a sudden shocking loss.

The Effect of Age and Sex on Grief

In our youth-oriented society it would be surprising to find that the death of an older person caused as much disturbance to the family or the community—apart from the mate—as did the loss of a younger person. This was not always so—for it is only the vast modern reduction in childhood and infant mortality that has forced mankind to think in terms of birth control to prevent the explosive overpopulation of our earth. In earlier times, when the death rates of young children and infants were sky-high nothing was thought of it—most children didn't grow up and the community just didn't and couldn't mourn that common an occurrence.

But our new way of looking at things has changed the attitude toward death. In line with this, Kalish found in his Los Angeles survey of ethnic differences that the great majority felt that the death of an adolescent or someone in middle age was a far greater tragedy than that of an old person. Kalish feels this reflects the idea that each person has a certain allotted life span, say sixty-five to seventy-five years, after which it is fitting to die. But the community also seems to be involved in a work ethic, and a man's death was considered more tragic than a woman's, and more so by women than by men simply because men are the chief providers for the family even now.

With this sort of thinking, it is not surprising to find that mourners respond in a similar fashion. Most studies seem to show that older people can accept the death of a mate more readily than the younger ones who show more grief in the form of physical problems.

The death of a young mate is seen as an untimely and therefore more shocking death. Geriatric psychiatrists feel the older woman is more likely to accept her husband's death simply because she is aware this happens to most older women. Most traumatic of all is the death of a child, or of the parent of a child. The dilemma of the widow is also unique. But these are all complex issues we will consider in detail in our later chapters. For now, let us turn to the deciding factors of grief that cause the most problems in mourning, and thus the most pain, and gain some help by knowing . . .

The Determinants of the Outcome of Grief

Certainly one of the most serious determinants of how mourning finally resolves itself is the person's background. The one who has lost a parent in preadolescent childhood is surely at risk, one who is likely to have difficulties with handling separations and losses later in life—and those who have lost parents in adolescence are also likely to have difficulties with these problems. But both of these are subjects for our in-depth exploration in the next chapter.

One indication of how mourning will be handled is how the person had handled other separations and losses throughout life. However, the loss of a grown child is unique, and Gorer believes it produces the most painful and longlasting grief. It's also been pointed out that in middle-class America the interdependence and closeness of the family is paid for in the pain of their separations, whether by divorce or moving to a distant home or death, formerly by being drafted into military service.

Not long ago, I heard someone remark: "Well, he hated his mother so it won't bother him when she dies." Sounds good, only it happens to work just the opposite way. The more ambivalence— the greater the anger in the usual love-hate relationship—felt toward the deceased, the worse the problems that arise. It's not the love that determines the intensity of the grief but the amount of hostility. Parkes, for example, found that among fourteen subjects who expressed ambivalence toward the deceased, eleven actually showed pathological grief. And Dr. Volkan has found that all his pathological grievers suffered a sudden loss. Another group that commonly runs into difficulties in their mourning is composed of those who have no opportunity to express their feelings, or whose background and emotional makeup is such that they find themselves unable to do so.

Another factor that we have already explored is the relationship of the deceased to the survivor. We've certainly referred enough to the problems of child and parental losses for young children being worst. Next come the losses of spouses, particularly husbands, although the loss of a wife causes the same degree of problems but isn't yet considered to be lifelong as with the loss of a husband.

The response to the loss of an adult's parents depends on a number of factors. For one thing there is the question of age—an elderly parent doesn't cause nearly as much disturbance as younger family members unless there is a good deal of ambivalence present. However, even if the parent was 103 and had been a vegetable for years, the death still causes grief and the stirring up of every separation problem the adult children ever had. Death and grief are always problems.

The loss of a sibling, a brother or sister, will result in a good deal more problems than those from losing an aged parent. For one thing there are almost invariably sibling rivalries with unconscious death wishes and probably anger that cause guilt feelings. Moreover, the death of a sibling presents a very personal and distinct threat—the "There but for the grace of God go I" feeling. For one's siblings are likely to be one's own age roughly, and so there is the personal threat of death. With this, too, goes the unconscious "Better him (or her) than me" feeling. While all this is perfectly human and normal, it gives rise to guilt and aggravates grief reactions.

But there is one devastating form of death for survivors.

Suicide and Its Survivors

Ordinary grief takes care of itself. The survivor will naturally heal by himself over a period of time if everything is as it should be, and rarely is the specialist used or needed. But in suicide, the survivor can become the victim as well, and for the family of the suicide, professional help (psychiatrist or clinical psychologist) is needed and should be utilized immediately following the death.

The severity of the shock of such an occurrence sets off a riot of tabooed thoughts, long repressed memories and bizarre wishes. The important survivor (say, husband or wife) would do well to seek help in the interest of the others involved, such as any children. The survivors find that the usual tearing feelings of acute grief are magnified and heightened by the terrible admixtures of shame and guilt and anger until they become obsessed by the thought that the death might have been prevented. The survivors may even see themselves as people who might have rescued the suicide or averted the tragedy—failures who all too often will punish themselves for this fantasied failing.

The family of victims of violence—murder or rape or even murder-rape—also need help, for these people are overwhelmed by the combination of violence and the most damaging type of death, the sudden one. The anger that is virtually always present in such survivors becomes outright rage which must be dealt with before it damages the family itself. These survivors should always seek professional help for the problems that invariably arise and can only be dealt with in a special situation by highly trained specialists.

Knowing the time frame of one's own grief helps immeasurably, for example, to provide comfort by just knowing that it's not unusual to feel grief in certain instances that lasts into the years. After all the first year really only brings back the normal energy levels of the bereaved while the grief itself goes on. Two or three years of grieving is not unusual, so survivors need not be disturbed—if the rest of the pattern is normal, and here we have offered yardsticks for measuring this. Anticipatory grief also catches many people unawares, and they may become worried and disturbed by the strange kaleidoscope that is grief. Knowledge here brings with it comfort and the hope for growth and change and a happier life.

But now let's turn to what we've already promised, the problems of grieving both for and by children.

CHAPTER SEVEN

Understanding and Help for the Special Bereaved: Children, Adolescents and Parents (death, divorce and disability)

> "Doctor, Doctor, will I die?
> Yes, my child, and so shall I."
>
> Nursery rhyme

Children and parents alike were once frank and open in talking about death, or this nursery rhyme would never have been written nor would it have lasted. Children still like it, and they at least are prepared to face up to its reality and honesty, even if the adults are no longer able to do the same. If one listens to the parents of twentieth-century America, one would think nobody dies anymore—all that people do is to "go away on a long trip" . . . "go to their eternal rest" . . . "fall asleep and not wake up" . . . "pass away" . . . "be taken up to heaven with God." The one thing modern Americans don't do, it would seem, is simply die! After all, ours *is* a death-denying society.

Yet as recently as the early part of this century, the adults were evading the issue of sex with their children, for then sex was taboo and adults felt certain that children had no sexual feelings and no sexual problems. The adults then believed that openly to discuss sexuality and conception and birth with children could only do them irreparable harm, because children couldn't possibly understand sex properly. Today, however, a long and stormy period of cultural reassessment, with final acceptance of the scientific insights of Freudian psychiatry, has resulted in the lifting of our sexual taboos to a very considerable extent.

Only now, strangely, this taboo has become attached to death, and today's adults now contend that children aren't concerned about or really aware of death, have little interest in it and no bereavement problems. Adults now are quite positive that children would only be disturbed by frankly admitting that there is such a thing as death and openly discussing it, which (it is currently believed) children couldn't understand properly anyhow. Yes all this does sound familiar, for that Victorian sexual taboo has been exorcised only to be shifted from one end of life to the other, sex freed and death brought under the same taboo.

Gorer's talk of the "pornography of death" thus gains added poignancy at a time when the stork carrying the baby has given way to the angel taking Daddy up to heaven (which today's adults with few exceptions don't really believe any more than they did that stork bit of yesteryear).

It's really only in the last half century that people have come to recognize fully how much damage the Victorian attitude toward sex has done to the young and so ultimately to the adults they grew to become. The casebooks of Sigmund Freud and his professional descendants right up to today are filled with the human tragedies and unhappiness that those sexual taboos eventually bred. But only a few observers yet recognize that our current death taboo is having tragic effects different in kind from the sexual ones, true, but similar in that they both have damaged first the young and then later the adults.

While most children who lose parents do manage to come through the experience—as most came through the sexual taboos without major psychic disturbances—the toll is distressingly high. Children are afraid to go to sleep ("Daddy has gone to sleep permanently"), steal, become behavior problems. Dr. H. Donald Dunton, Columbia University professor of psychiatry, tells of a six-year-old child who attempted suicide in order to join his own father up there in heaven because he pictured it as a fun life, a sort of eternal picnic, as it was explained to him by his mother. A show-business executive I know is still haunted—in his sixties—by the memory of how as a child he was lifted up and forced to kiss his dead father in the burial casket. Such mishandling of childhood bereavement is believed to be at the roots of a practice that has only recently become widely reported—the searching by adoptees for their real parents.

As the twig is bent so the tree will grow. What the child is taught about death will determine how he or she as an adult will deal with bereavement and separations of all kinds, and this teaching will affect all future growth and change. Evading children's questions about death only creates more problems for a variety of reasons we'll soon explore, because this way of dealing with the issue is only part of our widespread custom of death denial. Mrs. Marjorie Editha Mitchell, principal lecturer at a London college of education, tells how eighty-seven teachers in training were queried, and seventy-six of these felt that grown-ups evaded children's questions about death.

But in spite of the taboos and the mythology of our day, children and adolescents do grieve for parents and siblings who die. To recover, children, too, must go through the work of mourning, but in their own way which is unique and quite different from that of adults. Most psychiatrists, however, feel that true adult mourning is impossible before the age of eighteen. Then, too, there is the problem of divorce which represents loss and separation to adults and children alike, and both mourn it in their own way. Finally, there is the terrible problem of the child who dies (with all its torment for both parents and siblings), and even the difficulties that arise from the birth of a disabled or malformed child.

All these are topics we will cover in this chapter, for all are closely related and naturally fit together, since all lead to grief and mourning. More than anything else, however, this chapter will strive to provide useful information and understandings so that, should the need arise, these problems can be better handled.

At the very core of it all, the first area that must be understood is a fundamental one.

How the Child Looks at Death, and How to Help Him or Her Cope with It

"Bang—bang . . . you're dead!" Such death games are virtually universal among children, as are thoughts of death. But the small child has at best only a tenuous and insubstantial contact with reality. He readily turns to his private fantasy world which offers him a haven and a refuge, a place of escape when any real threat appears or when fears arise from his life situation or from change (the loss of a mother to death or hospitalization for example). Normal development provides increasing contact with reality as childhood fantasies are relinquished under the blanket of security the parents extend. But the child must learn to believe and trust, and this doesn't happen if he or she is lied to ("Daddy has gone away on a long trip," instead of frankly facing up to the fact that Daddy has died).

A child can easily be confused as he or she tries to learn about this great big new world. Isn't TV saying there is no death to its little addicts who see an actor killed on one program but alive and well on the next; see President Kennedy's funeral and burial, only to see him smiling and talking on a later program? While the child of pioneering days grew up in a harsh world with frequent violent deaths and stark simple burials in which he or she participated, he or she faced and learned the realities of life without confusion and accepted death as in the nursery rhyme—life and death went together and were accepted, neither was really feared. The result was maturation and alteration without the fear inherent in our death-denying and death-defying culture (for science and medicine work today to fight death and both talk glibly of living a hundred years or more).

There is still much argument among the behavioral scientists concerned with children about when the first full understanding of the concept of death occurs. Dr. John E. Schowalter, a Yale professor of pediatrics and psychiatry, believes that at about ten or eleven years of age the child has virtually an adult understanding of death's universal permanence. Although there is no complete agreement on the specific ages at which developmental changes take place in children and even some of the theories are still being questioned, the material here does provide a useful way of thinking about children and understanding them so that one can offer help to one's own offspring as well as others who may have the misfortune to suffer the death of someone close. And most authorities do agree on the approach suggested here as a way of preparing children for their lives which naturally are filled with the numerous normal separations and losses in the course of growth. Children, too, are certain to have their share of bereavements as they go on to become the adults and eventually even the aged persons of tomorrow.

It has been suggested that by the age of three months the infant is sufficiently aware of himself or herself and feels secure enough so that he or she can play peekaboo. If his or her face is covered with a cloth, the child will become slightly frantic until he or she finally catches the eye of the smiling mother and then relaxes, happily and smilingly. Dr. Adah Maurer, child psychiatrist, claims that the long-used word "peekaboo" actually comes from Old English words which mean "Alive or dead?" Maurer suggests that this simple nursery game may well be part of the child's learning about separation and death, as may also be the game of throwing a toy from the high chair and having the parent retrieve it. "All gone" is another favorite early childhood expression, and this too may be involved in this same learning experience of separation.

From six months until the age of two or three years, the child is aware of his or her caretaker (usually the mother), recognizes and is disturbed by separations from this person. Not until after six months does the child begin to recognize individual people—first mother, then father and siblings. Children also develop the capacity for longing about this time. Feelings of sadness and anger accompany this longing when the child is separated from the parent or other love object (whether parent or pet, toy or clothing). Now, too, the child begins to differentiate these feelings of sadness and anger.

During these first two or three years of life, adults can help the child to understand the difference between life and nonlife, that a chair or a toy is not alive and isn't going to feel anything, while a dog or a cat or a bird, another child or an adult, is alive and does have sensations. This is also the best time to teach a child about death, because he or she will accept it without upset, as just so much more information that he or she is avidly absorbing about this exciting new world all around.

Certainly, too, this child has had some brushes with death during everyday life—a dead insect or bird or worm or whatever. With the adult's help in understanding and absorbing this information, the child by the age of two or so can have formed a fairly concrete picture of death. By this time, too, the child should be able to deal with a more personal kind of death but one in which he has no immediate dependence such as with a parent—and so the child can accept and learn from deaths such as those of a grandparent who wasn't intimately involved with the child's care, a friend of the family or a playmate or a neighbor, a family pet such as a dog or a cat.

But this learning experience is only possible where the adults —parents or grandparents, say—are truthful and open in talking about the experience. Only a few generations ago when our society was honest and matter-of-fact about death, children could freely accept the reality of death, too. But today our society tries to deny death, and so adults approach the topic with a whole range of their own oft-confused emotional, philosophic and religious feelings. Until we have clarified our own feelings and are sure of what *we* believe and how *we* feel, we cannot convey a consistent, meaning-ful picture to a child.

Finally, the explanation must be set in terms that are appro-priate to the child's age and developmental level, explaining, for example, that the dead person won't be able to run or play or sing, can no longer feel happy or sad or laugh. The child just beginning school may well add, as one I heard did, "or go to school either," thus bringing the explanation right home to himself.

Religion here is a tricky thing to handle because young chil-dren really aren't equipped to cope with philosophic concepts or may be terrified. One youngster began to misbehave when he was told that "God took that child because he was so good," while another feared going to sleep because God took someone "in his sleep." The irrational and unrealistic explanations also cause trouble both from the fact that they are untruthful (and truth is the only way of dealing with a child) and because they can lead to all sorts of irrational fears. Thus it's not uncommon for children to develop sleep disturbances when they've been told death is a matter of "going to sleep"—or be terrified of travel when told that a dead person has "gone away."

Nor is it surprising that in a society as fearful and filled with denial of death as ours that its children should be disturbed by death. Here again is the importance of using death and grief as a means for growth and change, for this attitude cannot fail but help children to do the same. Out of this fear and denial of death come also the terrible haunting anxiety about aging that is so prominent a feature of America today. We don't have old people, only "senior citizens," again our technique of denial.

Only when we have learned to deal with separation and death will our children learn to grow old without fear and to face the trials of life honestly and openly, to turn life's necessary losses into gains and as the famous prayer says, "to change those things we can and to accept those we cannot change."

In this way, this preparation for life, we can soften the blow when as sometimes tragically happens a child must face death.

How the Child Reacts to the Loss of a Parent

The very young child is so totally helpless and dependent on its parents—its mother in particular—for everything it needs, for life itself, that any change represents a total threat to its security. To protect itself psychically, the small child shrinks into fantasy and withdraws to avoid the threatening reality.

Dr. Theodore B. Cohen, well-known psychiatrist and head of Pennsylvania's Committee for Mental Health Planning for Children, pointed out to me how separation and loss—"death is an extreme way of losing"—can be overwhelming to a child and even cost it its life. As he points out, the two-month-old child may respond to the loss of the mother or parents (through either death or hospitalization) with what seems to be minimal brain damage ("a failure of the central nervous system to move forward"). But at eight or nine months the child may respond "with something we call 'failure to thrive' marasmus, an acute depression which has a forty percent mortality."

As Dr. Cohen sums it up: "Each phase of the psychological development of the child has a different kind of grief or grieving for separation and loss. There is a fixation—the parent dies and the child stops moving forward in the area of object relations. The interrelationships of some of these people will remain shallow and hindered the rest of their lives."

There are a whole range of factors that determine the effects of the loss of a parent. The child's ability to cope with such a separation depends, of course, on age as we have just seen. The older the child, the more developed his or her personality and psyche, and so the less dependence on the parent, the better he or she is able to survive. Also, some children are more vulnerable than others, and this is a built-in personality factor just as is intelligence. Some children, too, mature faster than others.

Another important factor is the degree to which the parents have helped the child develop his or her realistic concepts of death, and this is one way in which parents can provide protection for their children against the possibility of their own death. This, of course, necessitates the recognition of the reality of our own mortality, a difficult thing at any time but doubly so in a death-denying society such as ours. The ability to do this depends in part on the parents' own parents and how they were helped to grow and cope with separation and loss as children.

The reaction of children to the death of a loved one (a parent in this instance) is very different from that of an adult. This response often creates problems of itself unless the remaining parent is sensitive to the child's reaction and prepared to handle it as well as his or her own feelings which are in none too good a shape at this point. A good deal of the child's reaction depends on what he or she has learned from the parents, whether he or she has been allowed, even encouraged, to express emotions (anger, anxiety, sorrow, whatever).

When children feel disturbed or distressed, they may show it in a whole range of changes that sometimes take a wise parent to recognize. There may be a difference in their usual cooperative attitude or in their moods, or there may be physical symptoms (pain, sleeping disturbances such as nightmares, feeding problems). There may be such very obvious things as a recurrence of bed-wetting or nail-biting or sudden lying about things, even stealing. Sometimes there is a longing, or a child may express anger or sadness or may be forlorn.

One of the most upsetting reactions to a bereaved parent is an apparent "lack of feeling" on the part of the child about the loss of the other parent. Yet what the surviving parent often forgets is that the attitude of the society and its adults will reinforce the child's own denial of the death. Moreover, the personality of the child imposes greater burdens on his or her coping with death than does that of an adult's.

The child, for example, has to cope with feelings of omnipotence and of magical powers. Depending on age and level of maturation, he or she believes that when he or she is angry with a parent or other person, when he or she has had death wishes either openly expressed or silently thought, these feelings have this magical power to kill, and so there is guilt about the parent's death. Actually this is often expressed in such questions as, "If I'd behaved myself, would Mummy have died?"

But again, so much of the details are variable that it's impossible to do more than indicate the range of reactions because children's responses are far more variable than adults'. And even adults respond to the death of a loved one with denial and disbelief, so it's not surprising that children do so very openly. One pattern often followed is simply to turn around and go outside to play. By getting involved in something familiar, children protect their psyche which is still immature and doesn't have all the protective defense mechanisms adults have developed.

To make matters even worse for the child, when one parent dies he or she really suffers a double loss, for the surviving parent, too, is lost emotionally under the best of conditions, since we've seen how adults suffer with the loss of a spouse.

But the chief concern of parents is . . .

How to Tell the Child and How to Help Him or Her Cope

Probably the key word here is honesty—with this, love for the child and some sensitivity, most things can be worked through successfully. However, professional help or even some advice (a psychiatrist or clinical psychologist) can be a big plus in this situation. A good deal also depends on whether there were other recent stresses, a sudden shocking type of death, any parental difficulties beforehand (illnesses, financial problems). Professional help is sometimes essential so that the surviving parent can cope with both his or her own problems as well as those of the child.

With so many parents acutely aware of their responsibilities for the child's emotional welfare, the survivor readily develops feelings of inadequacy and guilt. To make matters worse, the smaller the child, the more likely it is to react to the loss with anger over what it feels is desertion, by both parents, since one is gone and the other distraught and not as reactive as usual to the child.

The anticipated and the unexpected deaths must be handled differently with children. When there is no warning, it's best to consider how well the child has been introduced to death and how old he or she is, although the four-year-old may be more mature than the six-year one. If there is any doubt in the parent's mind, professional consultation should be sought. But avoiding the necessary confrontation (sending the child away for days or a week or two) is bad and so are the vague euphemisms so common ("Daddy's gone away on a trip").

The child might be given a chance to be prepared if the surviving parent says, "I have something very sad to tell you," and then does it in a sharing way. Young children are only confused by terrifying details or vague theories; it's best told simply at the child's age level and accompanied by the reassurance that the family will stick together, that the child will be cared for and whatever was done before for him or her will continue to be done (if the mother has died, daytime care will be arranged for, if the father, that moneys will be available, plus whatever special care the child associates with the lost parent).

All authorities agree that it is good that the child see the surviving parent's own honest sorrow and tears; this will help the child express his or her own grief and to mourn at his or her own level. What is told the child must fit the parent's own belief systems, religion for example. It is likely only to confuse the child for a parent to attempt to explain the death in terms of a religion he or she doesn't believe. The child will sense the underlying untruth and disbelief and this will only hinder communication rather than help.

When a parent has a long-drawn-out fatal illness, dealing with a child becomes more complicated, and authorities suggest a variety of approaches. Professional help may be vital here and should be used. For example, Mrs. Erna Furman, a Case Western Reserve University professor in child therapy, suggests the child be brought into the picture by being allowed to do something for the sick parent: any simple thing, even a visit or a gift of a picture drawn by the child, some flowers picked especially for the parent by the child.

But when to tell the child of the approaching death is not an easy decision. Many children pick up the situation and ask if the parent is going to die. Here the dying parent must be protected as must the relationship, so Mrs. Furman suggests telling the child perhaps that ''The doctor tells daddy (or mummy) . . . there are still things he or she can do,'' for example. When the parent is too sick for the child's visitations or phone calls, then one can say the doctor now says there is nothing further he or she can do but that the parent will be kept comfortable until he or she dies. At this point, parent and child can now grieve together in anticipation. But always there must be an emphasis on the fact that the child will be protected, needs met and everything kept as close as possible to what it was.

Dr. John E. Schowalter, a Yale University professor of pediatrics and psychiatry, advises that the younger the child, the simpler the explanation be made and the closer to the time of actual death.

If possible the dying parent might tell the child he or she is getting the very best of care, that he or she has no control over death but will stay alive as long as possible.

When death does take place, experts agree the child must be told gently but honestly, along with reassurances about his or her care and that all arrangements will be discussed as they are made and that the new, smaller family will go about its business of living. Professional advice is of inestimable value in preventing mistakes and making the surviving parent's double burden a little easier.

Funerals, Mourning and Children

Here, too, there seems considerable agreement among those most knowledgeable about the problem. The child's individuality must be reckoned with and professional help utilized. Dr. Robert A. Furman, director of the Cleveland Center for Research in Child Development, feels it wisest to allow a child to share in this family affair—but never to force him or her. He suggests explaining the whole thing in detail and leaving the final decision to the child.

Sometimes funeral services are modified to make participation helpful and not traumatic. The services, for example, might be shortened, the casket kept closed and no demand that the child touch or kiss the corpse. Dr. Furman suggests the best guide here is not to offend the child's sensibilities. Shiva for example might be modified to a simple form of visitation by friends and relatives during the days following the funeral.

The very young child who doesn't wish to attend the funeral or whose attendance would prove too great a load for the surviving spouse can sometimes be safely left home in the care of a familiar, trusted adult who can answer any questions and deal with the child's feelings. Professional advice is best because the surviving parent is so torn and confused that it is difficult for him or her objectively and sensitively to judge the child whose problems and needs are likely to add fuel to an already roaring fire.

The task of mourning is so great for the adult who has a lifetime of experience to draw upon, and presumably has already learned to go through separations, that we can only view with pity and awe the task forced upon a small child who loses a parent. For it is precisely when this child needs the support of both parents at their best that this child finds himself or herself with only one parent and that one limited by his or her own inner torment. At this time the adult tends to regress, needs to feel protected and comforted—and so does the child. It's a difficult period when professional help should be freely drawn upon. The assurance of continuing care and constant surroundings will help a child to mourn, and an understanding parent will respond on a flexible basis, knowing when to speak and when to remain silent, when to hold the child tightly and when to let him or her go off to be alone.

The success of the child's mourning is in many ways the measure of the parent's uniqueness, for it is a monumental task these two face, one the child can accomplish only with parental support and constant help.

Mrs. Judith Wallerstein, University of California at Berkeley School of Social Welfare, points out that children react in widely different ways: "There's considerable variation by age and by sex and by a whole variety of other factors. Some deny and others show feelings more openly. It all varies in terms of the individual child, who asks the child, what the environment encourages or discourages. In some instances there is a delayed grief response which doesn't mean it isn't a good response—and parents need to know that. In some instances a child is really working things out and not talking about it."

One of our leading experts in this area, Mrs. Wallerstein explains: "There has to be a coming to grips with it, but a lot of it takes its own time. . . . One cannot expect an immediate reaction from a child. . . . One has to give it a good six to nine months to see if there is any working through of the problem. . . . Our central criterion is whether there's a continuation of the child's development or whether the development is fixated.'' Sometimes only an expert can decide.

But parental loss isn't the only problem children face.

Grief for the Death of a Child's Sibling

Essentially the same principles apply as those we have already discussed, but there are a number of very special differences. Both parents are available and family continuity of care is assured, so the child starts from a better base when he or she loses a brother or sister than when he or she loses a parent. But there are other aggravating factors.

Under normal conditions, sibling rivalry is usually present, with its competitiveness, envy and anger, and it is likely to be most severe in the school-age child. As always, the greater the ambivalence and the greater the anger, the worse the guilt following death and the more stormy and difficult the task of mourning.

When there has been an illness of any length, other problems intrude as well. Siblings commonly compete for parents' love, which children measure by the attention accorded them, so any extra time given one sibling is resented by the other. A fatal chronic illness often leads parents to devote more time to the sick child, to allow more liberties, expect less and punish less. The well sibling feels shut out and less loved, turns envious and angry and expresses these feelings in wishes—expressed or unexpressed— that the sick child die. To a child, these wishes have magical power, so he or she feels he or she has killed the sibling when the latter dies.

Parents are now faced with the triple task of carrying out their own agonizing grief work while at the same time helping the surviving child in his mourning, and finally they must keep the family together and going about its business of continuing life. They have to reassure the living child that he or she had nothing to do with the death, and they have to accept such seemingly "terrible" behavior as the surviving child's normal reactions which may include open resentment at having plans interrupted by the death, demands for possessions of the dead child, a seeming coldness and total lack of sorrow.

It takes wise and strong parents to cope with all this, along with all the disturbances we mentioned in connection with parental death (sleep and eating problems, regressive behavior, such as bed-wetting, concern over personal death fears and fussing about minor ills).

Parents must reëstablish normal family life as soon as possible, a monumental task in itself for bereaved parents. Particularly they must avoid the danger of forcing the survivor to compensate them for the loss of the sibling ("You must be as good in school as your sister" sort of thing). The parents must also understand, accept and explain the child's reactions to the dead sibling so he or she can better deal with his or her own feelings ("Your wishes couldn't kill your brother—wishes never can"). Should there be fixation at any level—even long-lasting symptoms—professional help is needed. In fact such consultations at the start can be of material help in preventing problems.

But there is another problem where parents or siblings die.

The Adolescent Who Loses a Parent or Sibling

Adolescence is a period of storm and agony, a time of everything and a time of nothing. This is the period during which the child must become a man or a woman, complete the final separation from the parents. At one moment the parent is dealing with an independent near-adult and the next with a dependent child, a period of transition with enormous vacillation. As Dr. Cohen explains: "The normal adolescent is cutting his ties to the parent and doesn't even want to look like his parents—the dirty sneakers, for example. . . . They cut through the ties so that by the time they are eighteen they have gone through cutting off the various attachments to develop a sense of self and then can grieve for the death of the parent and really work this through." Most psychiatrists agree that the first real adult mourning is possible only when the child has reached eighteen years of age.

All of this confusion and turmoil leaves the adolescent particularly sensitive to the death of a parent. Even while he or she is fighting that parent and striving to break free, feeling full of hostility and criticism, there is still that parent to come home to for safety and protection. So when the parent of a teenager dies, the affect is doubly devastating—so much so that the adolescent may fight very hard to deny the death.

As Dr. Morris A. Wessel, a Yale professor of pediatrics, points out, the adolescent will, on the heels of the death of one of his or her parents, talk without end about the magnificent qualities of the dead parent (whom the youngster couldn't stand just a couple of weeks before). The teenager may even regress to childhood patterns, may reach out to a substitute—family friend or doctor or whomever—for the lost parent. The youngster is often likely to complain he or she has no pep, can't fall asleep, has lost his or her appetite, "can't get with it."

Adolescents, too, will grieve quite differently from the adult and may show only a very short period of sadness because they simply can't yet bear the weight of adult grief so they protect themselves with a happy-go-lucky attitude. Yet they find little joy in school or social contacts, lose interest in things and people. The surviving parent must be sensitive to this confused child bouncing between adult independence and childish dependence, deeply wounded but unable to grieve in a way that heals as does the adult.

A great deal of understanding is needed here because this is a crucial period for the teenager and his or her development must be watched. If he fails to move forward in his or her development, professional help should be promptly sought. Too close an attachment between adolescent and remaining parent—particularly one of the opposite sex—must be avoided, for it may hinder the completion of the normal grieving process. The adolescent is likely to show many of the usual grief patterns—sleep problems, behavioral ones (stealing can occur as a result of the anger felt at the loss), dreaming and the withdrawal we already mentioned as well as very individual reactions.

Professional consultation, particularly early in the process, may be immensely valuable and prevent complications. But there is another problem that is increasingly common today.

Divorce and Children

All those confronted with divorce—husband and wife and children—react to this as to any other major separation. The adults react in a manner determined by what they have learned about handling separation earlier in their lives, and in most cases the reaction is the typical grief response with the usual anger, guilt and all the rest. This can be pathological also, for if the person never learned to separate he or she will never remarry but remain tied to his or her mate even though there is a legal divorce.

Children react as they do to the death of a parent. If the adult has learned to grow with grief, then there will be a healthy response of the adult to another of life's major separations. But in divorce there may be more damage than in bereavement, because when there is a death, the community and friends show sympathy, offer help and in general try to support the bereaved. But in divorce, despite its frequency today, there is no protection, no customs or rites by which we recognize the death of a relationship, no way to prevent denial of its end, no ritualistic way to mourn a divorce.

Mrs. Wallerstein and her colleagues have conducted a divorce project and found that over 80 percent of the parents either didn't explain to their preschool children what was happening or gave them an explanation the children couldn't possibly deal with. As she puts it: "Somebody has to explain to parents how to explain things to children." A visit beforehand with a trained professional can make a world of difference to the children involved and to their future.

And now for the most traumatic of all grief. . .

The Plight of Parents Who Lose Children

The most permanent of all losses through death is the loss of children, for parents never really get over this. This is the most unnatural of all losses, an offense against Nature and a shock whose waves ripple out to affect parents, marriage, siblings, grandparents, and relatives and friends. One need only know a couple as I do whose school-age child dies suddenly to know the devastating nature of this insult to the scheme of all human life, this occurrence which turns life upside down, striking at the wrong end of life like some demented force whose only aim is destruction. From this, marriages are smashed and people die. It is one wind from which no good can possibly come.

With the sudden, the accidental or violent death, the shock is enormous, and I've known at least one bereaved mother who was saved from suicide only by the devotion and close care of husband and friends. For this loss there is nothing to say, except that it will never be forgotten, the grieving will last as long as the parents do. If there was any weakness in the marriage, it will break up.

But when parents are confronted by a virtual sentence of death on their child—an incurable cancer or other invariably fatal disease—the process is different. Totally numbing, the information is usually met by denial and disbelief which show themselves in a variety of ways. Parents are frequently amazed and even guilty about what seems to them a lack of feeling at the news. Actually this is a numbness as in initial grief which protects and makes functioning possible at such a time.

Most parents find someone they can let go with and virtually time their letting out so that it doesn't interfere with the necessary care for the child, the decisions that have to be made, and maintaining the stability of the child and other children. Dr. Edward H. Futterman, a University of Illinois professor of psychiatry, and his colleagues studied more than a hundred such families and were impressed by the way these parents handled their grieving so that they could carry out the necessary tasks of caring for their children, reaching out for support to others, whom they themselves selected, and even keeping their families on a level keel through it all.

In an attempt to understand, parents examine themselves and their behavior minutely, looking for something they may have done which could have resulted in the cancer or other illness. Guilt feelings are evident, as are the other emotions we've already seen: anger and hostility and all the rest. Since most such diseases are not acute but long-drawn-out affairs, the parents suffer anticipatory grief, but a very special kind. Their denial results in many requests for consultations with other doctors. Parents may often be allowed to participate in the care of the youngster and invariably become experts in the disease, reading everything they can about it and discussing each treatment or test with the doctors, often suggesting others.

To protect themselves, parents must gradually let go as must all grievers. There should be no guilt feelings about the normal responses that occur: wishing it were all over, getting involved with other interests and so on. Futterman and his team found that even while these parents were getting ready for the end, they were still doing everything they could in assuring the care and welfare of the child.

As this slow, long-drawn-out process winds down its fatal

way, parents develop a certain detachment and acceptance so that grief is mellowed and only flares up when there are relapses or some special occasion. There is an attempt to find some new philosophy so that life can go on, the other children be protected and enjoyed. Despite all the preparation, the final death is still painful, although the immediate reaction may be a mixture of relief and quiet sadness. Unknowing relatives or friends may even be reproachful that there are no tears or severe parental grief reaction at the moment of death. Nevertheless from here on, the work of mourning still needs completion—good grief must still follow, for the acute grief usually comes on the heels of the actual death.

However this process of anticipatory grief does make possible a life for parents and family after the tragic death of a child. When this process is possible, it obviously makes life and the necessary grieving much less stormy and painful than the tragedy of violent death which sometimes strikes.

As we will see in our next chapter, man's reaction to any loss is grief, so this response is involved in much of life. Another instance of this is a problem that afflicts the parents of a quarter-million American newborns every year.

The Plight of the Disabled Child

These infants are born with significant congenital or inherited abnormalities varying from Down's syndrome (mongolism) to harelips and cleft palates.

The parents of such children never cease sorrowing over the loss of "normality" in their children. This pattern follows closely the grief we have been probing, starting with the initial shock either after the birth or the recognition of the handicap. The awareness of this problem has come from a team headed by Dr. Mark Degnan, Albany Medical College of Albany, New York, which reports that such parents usually go through periods of denial "during which they will deny the diagnosis or deny their own feelings about the implications."

These parents exhibit both denial and disbelief, showing this in their shopping around for a physician who will tell them what they want to hear. Like all mourners, these see the problem but "fail to come to grips with its emotional implications." With the continued denial, it is clear these parents haven't worked out their grief response.

Instead of accepting reality and coming to terms with it, these parents develop guilt feelings because of their negative attitude toward their children. This guilt in turn leads them to overprotect the child which prevents his or her developing beyond the infantile level and in areas where he or she may be free of handicap. Professional help is clearly called for in this problem.

There are many aspects of grief and many problems tied in with it, so our next chapter might almost be regarded as a mélange of grief—aspects, problems and help all mixed together.

CHAPTER EIGHT

The Many Faces of Grief: Its Role in Sex and Widows, Pills, Aging and Retirement, Childbirth and Moving, Surgery

> One generation passeth away, and another generation cometh: but the earth abideth for ever.
>
> Ecclesiastes 1:4

Loss and separation and the grief they arouse are inextricably woven together into the fabric of life itself. Learn to conquer grief and you've gained control over life itself, for grief is ubiquitous: it's present in the good and the bad, the gains and the losses, in aging and in childbirth, it affects sex and surgery, it's there when you retire and every widow feels its heavy hand. Grief is the very stuff of life, and if we want to build a satisfying and happy life, we must learn to use it for growth and change. But all this is possible only when one learns to recognize grief in its many guises, for psychotherapy has shown that only by facing up to the real underlying problems can one hope to deal with them successfully, to do the necessary work of mourning when grief is that problem.

Here then are the many faces of grief, the problems they create and something of the ways to cope with them. But first a warning.

Pills and Grief: Protecting Yourself from the
Medical Drug-Pushers

Ours is a pill-popping society, and there are many experts who
lay this tragedy at the doors of the medical profession itself.
However this is a two-way street, and the public must recognize its
own responsibility here. It's been said that the only thing greater
than a patient's desire to have a physician who is a magician is that
physician's wish to be a magician. So we speak of antibiotics as
"miracle drugs," and doctors reach for their pens and Rx pads
faster than Marshal Matt Dillon on "Gunsmoke" ever reached for
his six-shooter.

Drug houses spend large fortunes for advertising mood-
altering drugs on radio and TV and in all the news media, in
medical, dental and psychiatric journals. The result is that Dr. Paul
D. Stolley, Johns Hopkins professor of epidemiology, has found
that nearly one in every five of all prescriptions given to patients
are for the psychoactive, the mood-altering or psychotropic, drugs
(tranquilizers, sedatives, sleep aids and the rest). With over two
billion Rx-dispensed in 1970 alone (and still increasing in numbers), that means some 350 million orders were filled for psychotropic medication. The public has been so brainwashed that people
expect to have a pill for everything from the "blahs" to the
"blues," to swallow something if one fails to go immediately to
sleep when one's head hits the pillow.

Our society wants to float along on a chemical pink cloud, and
psychoactive drugs are advertised to physicians in their journals,
urging such Rxs for children in school and older siblings leaving
home and going to college for the first time and having to cope with
a separation anxiety which is essential as an experience (needed for
growth and change, another lesson in handling the grief of separation and loss). Dr. Robert Seidenberg, State University of New
York professor of psychiatry, deplores this: "As a cigarette com-
mercial once told us to 'reach for a Lucky instead of a sweet,' we

are now in effect told to 'reach for a pill' instead of a thought!''

All too often, instead of giving the patient the time for sitting and talking out a problem, the physician pushes an Rx for a psychoactive drug across the desk and saves himself or herself some time, while the patient is too conditioned to pills to protest or question.

In 1970 alone the drug industry turned out five billion doses of tranquilizers, five million of barbiturates and three billion of amphetamines—and probably much more today. Dr. David C. Lewis, a Harvard professor of medicine, surveyed doctors and found two-thirds of them felt that other doctors were overprescribing psychoactive medication and over half the druggists questioned agreed that people themselves were buying too many over-the-counter mood drugs. Dr. Mitchell Rosenthal, well-known New York psychiatrist and drug expert, put it well: ''Treatment by drugs is substituted for treatment by people.''

Unfortunately the first things that are offered the bereaved are tranquilizers or other psychotropic drugs—either by physicians or by well-meaning friends and relatives—the usual reaction in a pill-popping society. But another drug that may have even more danger—and the most commonly used of all—is alcohol. The dangers inherent in all this are several.

For one thing, to smother grief chemically, burying it under a fog blanket of drugs, can prevent the grief work from being carried out and mean serious later problems in unresolved grief, the very difficulties we discussed in chapter 5. For another, there is the ever-present concern, particularly today, of addiction or drug dependency—and here alcohol is probably the worst offender. Finally there is an actual danger of suicide. Dr. Bruce L. Danto, a Wayne State University professor of psychiatry and suicide expert, points out that one of every three fatal suicides is accomplished with a drug prescribed by a doctor. As he emphasizes, the person suffering with anticipatory grief may get drugs—from physicians or friends or relations—instead of personal and emotional support. Dr. Danto warns of the potential suicide danger of making drugs available to both survivors-to-be and actual survivors of bereavement.

True, prescribing drugs for bereavement is nothing new, for Dr. Benjamin Rush, signer of the Declaration of Independence and surgeon general of the Continental Army, advised "liberal doses of opium" for grief, but hopefully we have learned something about medical care in the last two hundred years. Maddison has found very little proof that there is value for drugs in bereavement, has even found that those mourners who did poorly used significantly more psychoactive drugs.

The experts are in virtual unanimous agreement that drugs have at best only the most limited and temporary place in almost all grief and mourning. Parkes, too, questions the use of drugs in grief, and has found alcoholism a real threat, for more than 10 percent of the bereaved psychiatric patients he investigated in two studies did become chronic alcoholics. Dr. White, for example, advises against daytime psychoactive drugs and feels that the chemical calm of drugs can impede the working through of mourning. The use of very limited nighttime sedation, however, may be helpful when insomnia is a problem.

Probably the best summation is that of Dr. Castelnuovo-Tedesco: "Drugs haven't very much to offer in grief because the main issue is psychological and would have to be managed in psychotherapy, helping the person come to terms with the loss. You can't wish these feelings away chemically, although perhaps just for a few days it might be wise and helpful to cushion the acute shock."

But there are other problems to plague and worry mourners and one of the most disturbing is . . .

The Relationship Between Sex and Grief

Despite the very considerable lifting of the taboos on sex in our society today, psychotherapists still find that sex and death are the two most difficult things for people to bring themselves to talk about. Feelings about both obviously go to the very core of the human psyche, for they represent the two most basic drives of all animal life—reproduction and self-preservation. Man often tries to substitute one for the other: since he cannot live forever himself, he often attempts to go on living in the person of his offspring, even giving them his own name.

In the light of all this, it's not surprising how violent is the upset produced by the death of someone close, a reminder of our own mortality, a "there but for the grace of God go I" sort of thing. With the enormous turmoil and many emotional reactions in grief, it's really not surprising that sex should suffer for a number of different reasons. But these sexual disturbances cause the bereaved added anguish, unless he knows what is likely to happen and just what it all means. All of which is further proof of the importance of knowledge in order to relieve bereavement of some of its most disturbing elements.

Grief actually has a double-barreled effect in this area—not only does it change the mourner's attitudes and thinking about sex, but it also affects the basic sexual drive so that there are marked sexual changes at this time. This can create an atmosphere of near panic unless the individual (and the spouse or sexual partner where there is one) is aware that all this—like grief itself—is only a temporary state which Nature by itself will eventually restore to the normal or original situation. Like the rest of the bereavement process, sexual recovery, too, is a slow one of gradual healing and recovery.

One can almost divide the sexual reaction to grief into three areas depending on who has died, whether a spouse or other beloved sexual partner, a parent or some other loved person. Two reactions, however, that are common to all three deaths are emotional withdrawal, and loss of interest in all the sufferer's usual activities (one man I know who has been deeply interested in national and local politics for some forty years has barely glanced at the newspapers during the recent presidential campaign, has been virtually divorced from the whole thing for the first time in his adult life). This lack of interest simply spills over to include sexual activities as well as the other ones. The emotional withdrawal that goes along with grief also takes its toll on sexual activity with its intense affects.

The sexual aspects of grief are actually very complex and filled with a host of problems. For one thing, sex represents much more to the human being than simply a matter of satisfying physical needs—a mature sexual relationship also involves and provides emotional closeness and warmth, love and a feeling of being wanted, tenderness and security, pleasure and a wide range of other nonsexual but essential affects.

These rewards of sexual activity would be invaluable in grief were it not for the fact that engaging in sexual activity by supplying all these worthwhile and enjoyable emotional reactions can also produce guilt and anxiety and in turn these feelings lead to a reduction or loss of sexual activity. Then, too, the lack of sex only increases the very loneliness and emptiness that are so prominent a feature of grief and takes away from the sufferer the very considerable consolation and help that sex would offer. So the sexual problems in grief feed on themselves until we almost arrive at an insoluble situation, unless we recognize the situation and its passing nature.

To add to all these difficulties, problems also arise in any marital or sexual relationship at this time unless the partner, too, is well aware of what goes on inside the bereaved person. Thus, an unknowing partner may react to the sexual deprivation—or may react negatively to the sexual needs or expressions of the grieving person, misunderstanding and regarding these as ''improper at such a time,'' so that marital tensions can be added to all the other difficulties.

But along with all this reduced sexual desire and lessened interest in sex, there is an accompanying increase in the need for tender, warm and loving physical contacts with one's mate or sexual partner. An understanding partner can offer enormous help and support at this time both physically and emotionally, and under these circumstances the mourner will gradually come back to his normal sexual patterns. Slowly the relationship will be restored to what it was before the tragic loss occurred (and all losses are tragic).

This is not an easy period, for sexual behavior can be quite disturbed with a marked loss in some aspects and an increase in others. What would under ordinary circumstances be considered inadequacy or impotency or frigidity or whatever are really only symptoms of the basic underlying grief process. When these occur for the first time in a person during the bereavement period, they need cause no alarm, for they should disappear with the healing process, with the completion of the work of mourning. Like grief itself, the sexual problems, too, lift in a slow, irregular, episodic pattern.

It is when a mate is lost that the greatest disturbances in sexual behavior and patterns appear. The surviving mate feels the loneliness most sharply and with it an intense and even exaggerated desire for physical closeness and warmth and affection. The survivor—particularly a man—may be aware of this need as sexual desire, and a warm, supporting and comforting partner is sought. This process may represent from the psychiatric point of view a form of denial of the loss or an unconscious attempt at a reunion with the loved one.

However—and here is where the difficulties can be almost insurmountable until healing takes place—these feelings arouse intense guilt and anxieties. Particularly with the unconscious denial of the death of the mate, this desire for sex or the actual sex act may represent marital infidelity to the survivor. Here, survivors are caught between the Scylla of sexual and emotional needs, and the Charybdis of guilt and anxieties—ground between a rock and a stone.

In an attempt to solve this problem, some survivors repress their sexual feelings while others turn to a sexual act without love, or to masturbation, both of which also aggravate the guilt, the anxieties and the inner turmoil. Some may try to deal with all this by seeking out a series of substitutes for the lost valued person, and these survivors become promiscuous, while others may turn to drugs (sedatives, tranquilizers, barbiturates, alcohol) instead—the gay divorcée, for example. Dreams, too, take their toll of the bereaved with vivid, extremely disturbing nightmares, "wet dreams," or obviously sexual dreams of the deceased partner, all of which increase the normally heavy load of guilt and anxiety that the bereaved bears until the work of mourning is successfully completed.

Some mourners instead of seeking a series of substitutes for the dead partner will look for only one with whom sexual activity can be used to deny their loss and reassure them that they have not been abandoned. When this happens, remarriage occurs—and it's necessary to know that survivors behave this way in order to prevent the mistaken marriages that are made at a time when the bereaved is not capable of the rational selection of a mate. Such a major decision is best postponed until the work of grief is done and the bereaved is no longer swept along by the uncontrollable emotional storms and crosscurrents of the active grieving process.

During this stormy period sexually, mourners can only protect themselves by being aware of the situation, of its pitfalls and difficulties, of the changing reactions and feelings they're likely to experience. The most they can do is to try intellectually to avoid mistakes. It's helpful to keep open social and family relationships, to satisfy sexual needs as far as possible without creating undue emotional problems, and to try to form a new life without the beloved deceased.

Where a parent is lost, there may also be specific sexual problems for the adult children. There are, of course, the generalized sexual reactions to the death of a loved one such as we first described. But there are also complex psychic mechanisms at work here, for, as children, boys want to take Daddy's place with Mommy and girls that of Mommy with Daddy. The reactions really depend on how thoroughly these attachments and childhood fantasies were resolved as the child matured and grew.

Mrs. Pincus, for example, has found that adult children after the loss of a parent may react with an immediate change in sexuality, a need it would seem to move ahead, to mature and to become more potent. The adult children tended, she found, to assert themselves, to take the dead parent's place in the family, in the work sphere and in creativity.

When it is another loved one who has died—a sibling or child or friend—the sexual reaction will follow the basic patterns we first described. But the individual reaction will depend on whether the sibling, for example, might have been much older and been seen as a parental image; what sexual relationships on an unconscious level might exist with the other loved person. This is very personal and the reaction extremely individualistic with no general patterns as we could suggest with parents and mates.

Closely allied to this problem of sexuality is that of . . .

Grief and the Widow

Actually this is more a cultural problem than a personal one. So it is one that the individual can do rather little to resolve—one can only move society a little bit by oneself. This is a very deep-seated problem for mankind, for the special treatment of the widow goes far back into prehistory. Primitive tribes had fixed patterns of dealing with this situation, and while we no longer burn or bury our widows with their husbands, nor make them cover themselves with a mat to crawl along hidden in the shadows when they venture out, nor even make them knock on trees so that others can hear them coming and be able to avoid them, yet we still react in irrational ways to make widows' lives difficult and often unsatisfactory.

However, some of the problem of the individual widow may well be personal, too, for there are those who do make happy and satisfying lives. One of the problems is a simple matter of arithmetic. In the United States in 1973, there were some 15,500,000 single, married, widowed and divorced men eighteen years of age and older as compared to some 23,000,000 women in the same categories. The disproportion gets worse in the older age groups where there are the most widows, so that widowers are in great demand and have a much greater likelihood of remarriage.

One must speak of widows in two terms—as a group and as individuals—and the widow herself must accept responsibility for her own situation simply because only in this way can she hope to overcome some of the many problems of both grief and widowhood. In general, Western society widows tend to be a minority group facing discrimination, difficult economic circumstances and an inability to participate fully in a society which commonly regards her with fear and discomfort. All too often these women end up in what has been termed "a society of widows."

For one thing, the myth of the sexually insatiable widow has done a good deal of harm. As a result of this, men tend to make sexual advances toward widows, causing many of them to avoid social situations and creating difficulties in business. This in itself is likely to send a timid widow virtually into seclusion, although those who are self-assured and socially competent find ways of handling the problem once the work of mourning is over. However, it does lead to loss of some friends in that married women may avoid having good-looking widows to their houses for fear of losing their own husbands.

Maddison feels that the way certain widows regard the world about them as unhelpful may arise not from reality but from their own inner feelings and their anger being projected onto the world about them. While our society doesn't give a widow an easy row to hoe, many do it successfully and retain their true friends while making new ones as women and not as "widows." This necessitates the working through of grief which is of itself terribly hard and painful for the widow, but those who succeed of necessity have grown and changed, become wiser, more tolerant and compassionate human beings.

This way the widow can see the people she deals with as individuals filled with their own problems and shackled by the ties of the past which have limited them by the myths and fears that make them uncomfortable in the presence of the bereaved, frightened by the taboos of death and mourning, or reacting to stereotypes of the "widow." In fact many widows have become more competent and independent, stronger women who developed aspects of their personalities which were buried and forfeited in the typical marriages of our culture in which the wife is dependent, often lost in the husband's shadow.

Certainly a great deal can be done to protect the widow by developing a more structured and ritualized pattern to support her during her bereavement, and a more distinct valued role in the society into which she reemerges after the work of mourning is completed. Society should also look to a more realistic way of viewing its widows instead of following our folk myths so slavishly. Most of all, perhaps we might learn to react to widows as women whose husbands have died, no different from those whose husbands have not died or those who never had husbands. All this would no doubt necessitate a restructuring of our society (which could be a healthy thing if we do it with growth in mind and an understanding and compassion for human beings).

But difficult as women, and particularly widows, find their minority status, another sector of our population has an even worse time of it and needs the same help that widows do.

Loss and Grief in Age

We're talking here about what in 1973 were more than 21 million Americans sixty-five years of age and older, more than one in every ten of us, in fact—and the numbers and proportions will continue to grow, for we are increasingly successful in our death-defying techniques. Despite medical advances, however, the biological process of aging still goes on, and with it the things that make the older person uncomfortable when he or she looks in the mirror in the morning.

Despite the denial of aging in our youth-oriented society (we have no old people, only senior citizens), we all do age and get old (if we're fortunate enough to live that long). Americans are hoist on their own petards: they develop miracles of medical care to preserve and prolong life, strive to live longer than ever before, and then have a terrible need to deny they will or do get old.

There is no better proof of our need to learn to come to terms with loss and separation than the way we deal with aging. For if we can grow and change, can accept separation and loss and grief, we will be able to accept age and enjoy it instead of spending the extra years trying to find ways of denying we're older. When Americans pass forty or sixty-five or eighty, they turn to dyeing hair, wearing inappropriately youthful clothes, acting like teenagers (riding tricycles, for example), speaking of ''the boys'' and ''the girls,'' and using euphemisms to hide from age as we do from death. But it's all to no avail, for our society still discards and denigrates the aged regardless of their looks or actions.

Age realistically is a time of loss and separation, loss of hair quantitatively and qualitatively, loss of personal energy levels and sexual prowess, loss of physical prowess and actual muscle mass, and of health (arthritis and other chronic disorders of age), changes in skin texture and so on and on.

But our society offers its members only an emphasis on youth and beauty which makes the reality of aging even more difficult to accept. Just as there are no rites for the widow to help her mark her loss and provide support, so there is no culturally accepted and recognized method of mourning for the real loss of youth and all it means and provides.

By learning to work through grief, through loss and separation, we can also learn to cope with age. For in old age we must grieve for ourselves and for what we have lost: strength and beauty and, before too long, life itself. Only if we have learned to deal success-fully with life's innumerable separations, can we do so with those of aging, too.

I have met many in their eighties who can realistically talk of what they've lost and the limited life ahead, and yet be happy. It can't be thus if we spend our old age trying to deny our losses, acting young to fool others as well as ourselves and never succeed-ing. As in mourning, only when we accept the reality of the loss can we go on to build a satisfactory life, and in a sense we *can* stay young if we recognize the test of youth as the ability to grow and change, to remain flexible, and this in itself promises new satisfac-tions and new interests and new rewards as long as we live.

Closely akin to this aging is the problem of . . .

The Loss That Is Retirement

Americans are being retired today at ever earlier ages and being destroyed, for few Americans are prepared to recognize the reality and the trauma that is retirement. Instead there is that fantasy of the "young" senior citizens riding into the sunset of their golden years hand in hand and happy with their lot. Actually retirement finds most Americans ill-prepared to deal with this cultural recognition of the supposedly tragic loss of youth, the reality of the loss of social status, family importance, place in the community—for all these are lost in our function-oriented society where only those who produce material things are valued, and so can value themselves and retain their self-esteem.

The retiree faces a stirring up of the problems of his or her whole lifetime—all the losses and separations he or she ever failed to work out, for he or she is now separating from a job in a company where he or she has typically spent many decades of his or her life. Unless he or she is prepared to develop and alter, to move into other new meaningful work, he or she faces an empty daily round of doing nothing or of sports and/or games.

Actually the retiree should have some way of dealing with the losses of his or her new status: the social contacts at the office or plant, the meaningful role in the society of productive people, the problems of aging now emphasized by retirement. With an ability to separate goes a flexibility so that one can deal creatively with this new loss instead of living in the past—''When I was running that business,'' ''When I handled accounts we did it. . . .'' Those who can handle their losses move on to new fields—one professional man I know turned to breeding poodles, another business executive is in real estate, a third owns his own nursery. These men *do* stay young, but they have all turned loss into gain, grief into growth.

But loss starts at the other end of life's spectrum.

The Grief of Childbirth

The woman who becomes pregnant carries within her for nine months a new life. During that time she becomes dependent on her husband who in turn cares for her more than usual (the tradition of the strawberries in the middle of the night, anything the pregnant woman desires). There is also a feeling of fullness and well-being that goes with pregnancy.

On childbirth the woman symbolically loses a part of herself, her child, as well as the position of importance and the special attention that goes with pregnancy. Instead of being dependent, she in turn has an infant now dependent on her. As with all loss and resulting grief, the mother will mourn and the result is the postpartum depression—"the blues"—so often seen several days after childbirth and which many experts consider much more frequent than is actually recorded in hospital files.

Dr. Rudolph Toch, Harvard instructor in pediatrics, calls attention to a new problem in pediatrics. The altered patterns of sexual activity have led to increasing numbers of unwed pregnant adolescents, many of whom go through a grief more complex than that caused by the death of either parent or sibling. These girls who want abortions seemingly suffer little or no lasting emotional damage, Dr. Toch believes. But those children who press their own immature and unrealistic arguments for keeping their babies (even though they're only thirteen years of age) but have abortions anyhow, have excessive grief reactions. The worst of the grief problems appear in those who do have their babies, only to give them up for adoption. Toch feels that the loss of a baby in adoption is one trauma the mother never overcomes.

And finally there is the problem of bereavement from . . .

The Grief of Surgery, the Loss of Parts

Loss of a body part or organ through surgery results in an emotional reaction whose severity depends on the significance of the part (removal of a leg causes more reaction than that of a tooth, a mastectomy produces profound affects, since Americans idealize breasts which symbolize the woman's sexuality). Reactions vary widely depending on a whole series of psychological factors such as how the individual views the part involved (arthritis disfiguring fingers and hands has one meaning, a leg amputation another), what connections these have to past losses and how the individual has learned to come to terms with the separations and losses during his or her whole lifetime.

Once more we find ourselves facing the importance of learning to deal with grief, with separation and loss, to grow and change, for every operation is likely to cause the patient to mourn the loss of a body part. The extent of the problem is clear from the fact that there are, some say, as many as twenty million operations every year in the United States, and all of these have the potentiality of producing grief reactions.

Probably America's leading psychiatric expert on the losses of body parts and organs, Dr. Castelnuovo-Tedesco sums up this whole problem: "You are faced with the issue of loss throughout life, and it has to be dealt with over and over again. But one of the losses that is very difficult for people to deal with is the loss of organs. This leaves both sadness and a great deal of resentment associated with the loss. Organs tend to represent relationships and people in someone's experience, and also they of course represent the integrity of the body."

As the Vanderbilt University professor of psychiatry sees the whole picture: "All of us would like to feel we are somehow capable of stemming the tide of aging, accidents and all sorts of dire events which can overtake us—and finally and ultimately the death of the organism which represents the full obliteration of the self. Losses of parts of the body as well as the losses of other people remind us of our own mortality and our own vulnerability —questions which are difficult for anyone to think about in any clear or protracted kind of way. But the issue of loss essentially contains some or all of these questions."

So now let us turn to the actual how-to part of this book, the specific suggestions for help.

PART III
THE SPECIFIC HELP
FOR YOUR GRIEF

How to Help the Bereaved: What to Say and to Do, How to Tell When There Is a Problem, Whom to Turn to for Comfort

> "It is not good that the man should be alone;"
> Genesis 2:18

"I've had it with God and His will and His heaven. . . . If anybody else mentions them to me again, I'll . . . ," and the middle-aged widow whose husband had died very suddenly put her head on the table and wept. This happened well before I had begun the research into this book, and I was frankly shocked, although I wouldn't be today with what I now know about grief. For actually this sort of explosion is not only common, but this was a very mild one—most often these are directed at the very clergymen reaching out to help. Experienced, compassionate ministers today are neither startled nor shocked at this sort of outburst. They recognize that such remarks come out of the terrible pain and torment of initial grief, and the clergymen simply hear out the sufferers who often say far more outrageous things about God and religion.

Dr. Robert E. Kavanaugh—ex-priest, teacher and University of California psychologist—recalls how as a young priest at his first solo wake he approached the widow with a "How are you?"—to be met with, "How in hell do you think I am" from a tormented widow left with four children when her husband suddenly died. And Rev. Carleton J. Sweetser recalls how, at his St. Luke's Hospital in New York, he met a young woman who kept smiling widely all the time she was talking of the unexpected death of her young husband, or the pair of young men who tried to beat up the medical staff of the intensive-care unit where their brother had just died following an auto accident.

These are the sorts of problems that clergymen—and you and I—often face in dealing with the bereaved in ordinary, everyday life. For as we have seen, the affects of grief are so overwhelming that they often break down all the usual controls and functioning of human beings. Nevertheless, all of us do want to help friends and loved ones who suffer bereavement, whether it's a spouse who has lost a brother or sister or parent, a friend who has lost a mate or a child or whatever. This chapter attempts to offer ways by which you can help the bereaved: what to say and to do and when. Here, too, are suggestions for telling when there's a grief problem in the offing and professional help should be sought, and to whom a mourner can turn for help both in the everyday world of family and friends, and the specialized land of the professional expert. Let's start with . . .

What to Do When You Hear Someone You Care for Is Bereaved

First off, get in touch with him or her. Telephone and find out if you can see the mourner and arrange to drop in as soon as it's convenient, but let him or her know you are there and you want to help. Ask the mourner—or someone who's close to the situation or a relative—what you can do. The old-fashioned system was a good one: someone would always be with the bereaved and one visitor wouldn't leave until the next one arrived so that throughout the initial grief stage the bereaved was never alone. Such support and caring are important; just sitting and holding hands is enough.

The traditional visitors brought food and relieved the mourner of all tasks, whether caring for the children or cooking or shopping or whatever. Today this may involve answering the phone, greeting visitors, helping with needed arrangements. The "waking" or "sitting shiva" or other old customs were valuable, for they cared for the mourner during the initial days or week until the bereaved was able to take over his or her own responsibilities. The old rituals prescribed what was to be done and so relieved both mourner and visitor of embarrassment and awkwardness—their roles were clearly defined and everyone knew what to do.

Not many adhere to such customs in America today, so those who want to help are often held back by fear of saying or doing something improperly or clumsily. This really need not hinder you, for if you simply express your affection for the mourner, and for the deceased if you felt that way too, that is more than enough and is more helpful than anything else. It is your sincere feelings that are comforting and supportive at a time when these are badly needed. It's not what you say but how you really feel that matters.

It may be just as well not to say anything if you don't feel up to it—just to put your arm around the grieving person and allow him or her to cry on your shoulder or with you will be of enormous help and value. In our society we have forgotten the importance of and help given from simple physical contact, the equivalent of the "laying on of hands" (such an important element in healing).

Friends knowing of this book often ask me . . .

When Should You Visit the Newly Bereaved?

The Orthodox Jewish tradition is not to visit until after the funeral, to permit the mourners to be alone with the deceased and the close family, and this is good psychology. This gives the bereaved a chance to get over the initial shock with its numbness, confusion and anger. And during the time the body is on view or the funeral services—traditionally the time of visitation in the United States—there probably should be little said beyond a word or two of greeting and affection or simply pressing the hand or a short hug. The real communication must come after the burial.

What Do You Say to the Freshly Bereaved Person?

Let's start with what you should *not* say!

Sensitive clergymen today consistently shrink from the "God is good" . . . "It's God's will" . . . "Don't grieve, he's in heaven now" . . . kind of approach. Unless you know the mourner *very* intimately and are *absolutely* certain that he or she will respond positively to this approach, don't use it or you're likely to get the sort of answer with which we began this chapter, or much worse. The numbed, dazed mourner—filled with pain and sense of loss, angry with the world for taking the loved one away—is likely to explode at these stock phrases of what is more religiosity than religion. You will only hurt and not help with this sort of thing.

In fact, the trite phrases and clichés ("It's all for the best" . . . "He's out of pain now" . . . "He lived a good life" . . .) should always be avoided. If you can't readily and simply express your true feelings, don't say anything—just an "I'm sorry" will help, if it's sincerely meant. Many of those most knowledgeable about this—the clergymen—will say nothing, just hold a hand or put an arm about the shoulders and let their feelings of sorrow mingle with those of the mourner. If you don't really feel sorrow and concern for the bereaved, you're better off not visiting at this time.

It's disturbing and angering to a mourner—filled with pain and torment and thoughts about the deceased—to have people come in, murmur a word or two of sympathy and then turn aside to get involved in long discussions of the weather or the World Series or the stock market. Don't try to distract the bereaved with such topics either. I resented that sort of thing and I haven't met a mourner who didn't. If you can't handle any of the positive things I will shortly suggest, just express your sympathy and leave. Your very willingness to give up your time and make the effort of coming is helpful to the mourner and appreciated.

First off, don't take the lead—let the bereaved person set the pace and tone of any conversation. Some mourners are more comfortable when controlling their emotions and not talking about the deceased, although this is not common. Most mourners in the early stages want to talk about the one who is dead, and this helps them to accept the fact that the person is really gone, to begin to talk of the deceased in terms of "was" rather than "is."

What the bereaved needs when the funeral is over and a new life must begin varies. When there is still a spouse, he or she will carry the greater part of the burden, but there are many things spouses may not be able to do. For example, a husband may have to be at work and there may be small children to be cared for.

Particularly for the widowed, the friend or relative who makes no demands on the bereaved but quietly comes and takes over the routine essentials of the day-to-day management of the household is the ultimate in help for the bereaved—the person who does the shopping and cooking, sees that the needs of the children are attended to, that the house is kept in shape, the phone answered, those who visit are greeted. Most of all this means love and comforting to the bereaved, a sense of being wanted and needed, a chance to regress into dependency and have some of the terrible emptiness filled.

Then there are those who come to call but because of other commitments (home, families, businesses) have only limited time or personal capacities—these can offer a different but still needed form of help. For the bereaved also need those who are willing to sit and listen, and only sometimes to talk—most important of all here is to be accepting of *whatever* feelings the bereaved may express and in this way to reassure.

Those who visit and those who work, alike must be prepared to share the pain of the mourner, to accept the anger and tormented feelings as they come out. Feelings must not be dammed up, nor should the mourner be reproached for reactions—"You shouldn't cry" . . . "You mustn't say that, it's God's will" . . . and the like. Visitors can also help by letting their own feelings out; if they cry with the bereaved, both will be relieved and helped by sharing a mutual loss. And while the mourner must be free to talk of whatever he or she wishes, it is good for the visitors to talk of the deceased, of the warm moments and work done together.

Done in a warm compassionate way as the mourning moves along, some philosophic understandings may eventually be introduced to help the mourner pull the whole thing together, to begin to make some sense out of the death—and the life—of the deceased. But this takes very sensitive, subtle handling, not with clichés but with seriously thought-out views in line with the thinking and belief systems of the mourner. Praying together is of considerable help to religious people, once the initial anger with God and religion and the world begins to fade. In fact, anything that can be shared is valuable—tears, incidents involving the dead, feelings and thoughts—because they give the bereaved a feeling of being understood and wanted, relieve the sense of loss and emptiness and isolation which plague the mourner.

Knowing both the patterns of mourning (as we've already detailed them) and the individual can provide another help. For example, we've seen the "bad times"—awakening in the morning, the time the spouse returns home from work or a child from school, perhaps some such things as going out on Saturday evening or a Sunday afternoon. Even just a telephone call at the daily bad times or during the long empty evenings can provide a great deal of help by reassuring the mourner that he or she is not abandoned but still remembered and cared for. A visit or a joint involvement (say going to a museum on those Sunday afternoons, having the bereaved over to your house on Saturday evenings, going to a show together) done on a regular basis helps, and the regular part should be emphasized here.

Talking about the survivor's grief reactions can help, too. With the information from this book, for example, the bereaved can be reassured about their seemingly bizarre and certainly powerful and frightening grief responses and feelings. Knowing that their reactions are perfectly normal is both encouraging and heartening, the sort of thing that makes it possible for the mourner to face the strange patterns of grief without the panic that some manifestations such as hallucinations can cause.

In our society there is no official end to mourning as certain religious or folk rites offer. This, too, may become the task of the friend—to indicate that grieving should end after a suitable time. We now know that a year or so is a good period for ordinary grief. But what of the mourner, to whom can and should he or she turn for all this help? Where can these people find . . .

Who Is Best for Support?

Help comes for the bereaved from a variety of sources, and knowing where to look for it is obviously of value. The major studies have been directed to the problems of widows and, secondly, of widowers. Yet the experiences of these two groups is pretty much true also of other mourners, just as their grief is similar.

Many unfavorable things have been said about undertakers in recent years: they have been accused of taking financial advantage of the bereaved when these people were in no position or condition to deal with high-selling pressure or unscrupulous business people or professionals. However, the widows in the Harvard Study—one of the most extensive of all investigations of bereavement—found undertakers most helpful, as did London widows and those in a St.

Louis study by Clayton and her associates. The minister, lawyer and insurance agent all proved helpful, too, as did parents and children, but siblings and in-laws were not as helpful as close friends or even neighbors. Physicians trailed along at the end of the list, perhaps because the doctors had to be sought out and didn't enter the picture by themselves of their own accord.

There was a sudden initial appearance of a large group to offer support and interest—family, friends, co-workers of the deceased. However, once the funeral was over these usually faded quite quickly, since a large part of them were there to show their feelings not for the widow but for her dead husband. What was left afterward were close family and personal friends. And there might likely be problems with a mother-in-law: a "It was *my son* who died" sort of attitude that created a great deal of friction.

Three-quarters of the Boston widows found family more helpful than friends, and the women relatives proved the most valuable here. Mothers, sisters and sisters-in-law, even cousins and aunts, close women friends and neighbors saw to running the household, from food to chores and the care of the children. One of these women always stayed with the widow as long as was thought necessary. For advice and support, almost all the widows turned to their husband's brother (where one was available)—this one was the first informed of the death and the one who made many of the decisions from funeral arrangements to financial matters and even about the children. This brother-in-law setup, which was even followed by the widows of President Kennedy and his brother Robert after the two assassinations, may well be a cultural pattern.

The Boston widowers also needed help, and this too fell on the women, since what was most needed here were the household tasks: buying and preparing food, caring for the house and guests, providing for the children. But widowers on the whole also found funeral directors helpful. The women who helped here, though, were chiefly family.

However, professional help is available and should be utilized much more than it is. Ministers today have considerable training in pastoral psychology and in most cases can help a good deal. Medical care, too, should be utilized since there is considerable illness following bereavement. Thorough physical examinations may reveal disorders right at their very beginning and prevent their development into something much more serious. Physicians, too, are being indoctrinated in the care of emotional health problems and a competent doctor can be of considerable value, if he doesn't push pills but tries to offer "talking cures" rather than drugs, which have only slight value in the mourning process (even then only for a very short time under limited conditions except in unusual circumstances).

A great deal of help, though, is available today through the exploration of the myriad emotional problems that accompany grief. For this there are a variety of social workers, clinical psychologists, and, most importantly, psychiatrists. These professionals are particularly valuable when young children or even teenagers are involved in bereavement—and for the aged who lose spouses whom they will never be able to replace and who have limited social networks anyhow.

One of the greatest services friends or family can offer is . . .

How to Tell When There Is a Problem with Grieving

Essentially one can tell the normality of the grief process by comparing it with the good grief discussed in chapter 3 or the patterns of inadequate grief in chapter 4. We will just touch on the more obvious highlights here.

Certainly one of the outstanding features of normal grief is the way it heals itself. The numb, confused initial stage lasts no more than a week or so. Acute grief slowly moves toward resolution over the first six months after peaking during the first month or so with the crying, sleep disturbances, loss of interest and anger, painful longing and all the rest. As the first six months pass and time moves toward the end of the first year after the death, the mourner moves along on the way to resolution of the process—his or her ability to function increases while the episodes of disturbance decrease in number and length.

In short, what one looks for is whether the grief process progresses (however erratically and episodically) toward restitution so that by the end of the first year or so the energy levels are now approximately normal. At least for widows and widowers—and likely others, too—the process may go on for two years and perhaps three. But after the first year one's functioning should be virtually normal—the episodes of grief and sadness should be fewer and shorter with less effect on the way the bereaved goes about his or her daily affairs and business.

Professional help is needed should the grief process bog down, fixate, at any level—say, the mourner becomes unable to accept the reality of the death of the loved one and continues to deny it; or perhaps the acute grieving continues for more than a year or so to an extent where normal functioning is still not possible. Another example of stalled healing is where the mourner refuses to change things but, like Queen Victoria, keeps everything as it was when the loved one died and turns the home into a virtual shrine to the deceased.

Another warning signal is when there is *no* real grieving. Should the mourner show little or no emotion even at the start, no tears or crying or the rest, but be deeply involved with funeral details but no emotional involvement, professional help is called for. The same is true of any marked alterations in the quality or quantity of normal grief.

Another indication for medical or psychological care is when physical illnesses are of the type associated with stress: stomach ulcers or hypertension, certain skin conditions as hives, rheumatoid arthritis or any of those we already discussed earlier in this book.

Professional intervention is needed when there is too much or too little grief or when the process starts and then stops, or in any mourning that doesn't carry through to completion in one or two, or at the most three, years. Sometimes only a few visits with a psychotherapist are all that are necessary to deal with a crisis, without the long-term psychotherapy needed for some serious emotional problems. But if help is necessary it warrants seeking, for the whole rest of the life of the bereaved is at stake here. A failure to work out grief may well cost the mourner his or her chance for a happy, fulfilling life.

When there is any question, a consultation at least is well worth considering. And this may be particularly useful in order to prevent problems when a child's or adolescent's parent or sibling dies. A little advice and guidance may make the difference between normal grieving and serious emotional problems by providing the parent with the necessary tools with which to deal with such a child.

And now for our next and last chapter where we will explore the road back, the way the bereaved recover and how they can make it easy and successful for themselves.

CHAPTER TEN

The Road Back: Growth and Recovery, Avoiding the Mistakes, the Organizations That Can Help

> Life must go on;
> I forget just why.
>
> Edna St. Vincent Millay, "Lament"

Those who lose loved ones find themselves in a new and lonely universe which suddenly has been emptied of much of its meaning. But this new world is also filled with numbness and pain and confusion, with bizarre sensations and uncontrollable emotions, with overwhelming and often meaningless anger and guilt. Sometimes it seems a bottomless pit of black despair, where all is sorrowful desolation and unutterable torment. Yet there is a road back, long and lonely, traversing dark and unexplored territories of the mind. While most people do eventually find this road by themselves, there are ways to lessen the suffering, to make the journey back less frightening and less painful and more bearable.

How can grief bring growth, out of loss come gain? Loss and grief teach us the finiteness of life and the importance of time, press us to put every moment to worthwhile use, to enjoy and appreciate life to its fullest, to make the most of every relationship, every beauty, every value, even to spur us on to contribute the very most we ourselves can while we still can, to this world and to the people in it. The tremendous emotional upheaval that follows the death of someone close virtually forces us to reassess our entire life from a wholly new perspective, produces a change we can turn into growth if we will. While there can be no real growth without grief, no gains without losses, another odd thing happens—when the growth once starts, there is no stopping it, any more than you can stop the child or the teenager from maturing physically.

And this last chapter is to look specifically at that long way out of the depths of despair, the path to travel back from the abyss that is bereavement. True, grief work is a very personal thing and each of us must find his own way, as George Burns told *Newsweek* recently, about his own grief problem and its solution. When Gracie Allen (remember the comedy husband-wife team of Burns and Allen?) died after thirty-eight years of a marriage so close that it involved both their personal and their professional lives, Burns was so deeply shaken that he could no longer get to sleep. During the last few years of their marriage Gracie's bad heart necessitated separate beds. Unable to sleep one night after her death, George Burns moved over into Gracie's bed, and promptly went to sleep. True, one might speculate that this was a form of denial, of reunion with his beloved wife.

But just like George Burns, each mourner must find his or her own individual turning point, that change that makes possible the start on the way back, the conquest of some problem in the grieving. One professional man I knew was haunted by the thought of his dead father lying in the ground in all kinds of weather. It suddenly occurred to him that his religious father was now with his God—that thought relieved the man's anxieties, and he felt comfortable about the death.

This turning point is the symbolization of the mourner's meal to the Orthodox Jew (the need for the mourner to resume his life and his or her relationships, since the burial was now behind). The wake and the giving up of widow's weeds have a similar symbolic meaning—the reinvolvement of the mourner in the world about him or her.

But perhaps the most important thing the mourner must learn in order to travel the road back successfully is the lesson embodied in . . .

"The Talking Cure"

Dr. Josef Breuer, a Viennese physician and physiologist, discovered in 1880 that he was able to relieve the emotional problems of the patient he named ''Anna O.'' who had developed a series of physical symptoms (headaches, paralysis, and the like) during her father's fatal illness. These worsened with the father's death, but Breuer discovered that when Anna talked about the emotional problems underlying her symptoms, they were relieved. The Viennese physician concluded that neurotic symptoms arose from unconscious mental processes and would disappear when these become conscious.

Breuer never treated any other patient with his psychotherapy, but a few years later he did tell another Viennese physician (Sigmund Freud) about both his technique and his results. Out of this grew psychoanalysis, for Freud recognized the importance of ''the talking cure'' and developed the technique into his own psychotherapeutic system which eventually revolutionized all medicine, psychiatry and behavioral sciences.

Mourners can utilize the knowledge of the talking cure in their own grief in a very real and concrete fashion. The bereaved who bury their feelings—the anger, guilt, sorrow and the rest—are in for serious trouble. As with any other emotions, denial or repression merely dam up the unresolved feelings that sooner or later come back to haunt the person in a variety of ways.

The lesson of the talking cure is simple: that feelings should be expressed. Thus the bereaved who behaves in a manner our society approves (''The widow was wonderful—she never cried'') will make people happy by not embarrassing them or making them confront their own buried feelings, but she will be laying the seeds for inadequate or uncompleted mourning and serious trouble for herself later on.

The mourner who wants to find the road back must express his or her feelings openly—there must be weeping and wailing, anger expressed in an appropriate manner (it's good to say how mad one is at the world, not good to have a fight with the boss or punch someone). Guilt feelings have to be faced up to, along with many other feelings. Everyone goes through these emotions, but only those who can talk them out emerge not only unscarred, but also as a richer, more understanding and compassionate person. The person who fails to express his or her feelings ends up like a heated kettle which can't blow off steam and finally builds up the inner pressures until it just simply explodes—there has to be a vent, a safety valve.

The best way to sum it all up is in Dr. Volkan's words to me: "If I were to give advice to people, this is what I would say: it is not a shameful thing to grieve, to cry out, to feel angry or disturbed or as if something has been torn away from you. You feel helpless for a while and you want to fight the whole world, to strike out, or you want to cry."

The University of Virginia professor of psychiatry stopped for a moment, thought and then went on to sum it all up: "I think people should know about this, because the sterile way of dealing with grief is possibly going to bring some problems—these feelings of loss, of anger and helplessness, wishing to cry or strike out—these kinds of feelings are very human kinds of things. Grieving is a loss—a very, very private thing. Nobody can grieve for another person, but the grieving person needs to know that he or she is not alone."

But now let us see how this can be used at the various stages.

The Initial Phase of the Mourning Trail

This is the first week or less, the time of the wake and of shiva. During this time the mourner is in shock and numb, so involved in the struggle to keep head above water that there is little energy left for recovery. Emotions and behavior are virtually out of control under normal circumstances—disbelief and denial, weeping and wailing all mix together with shock so that most sufferers afterward have only a vague remembrance of the experience, protectively dim and disoriented. All one can really do is as a famous French abbé said when asked what he did during the French Revolution: "I survived!"

The best thing the mourner can do is to let it all hang out, to show his or her feelings and grief unashamedly. Significantly, Maddison found that the widows with the greatest health problems felt they had not been allowed to talk about the death of their husbands or to let out their feelings freely.

However the period is such a short one, and people do recognize that the mourner during this time "isn't himself" (or herself) so that there is some understanding, because one's lack of control can and does create problems for the future. Fights during this time can destroy lifelong friendships, create difficulties with family and the like. It's also a time when no major decision should ever be made: buying or selling a house, business moves or whatever. One can only try to keep control by awareness of what goes on at this time. But in the next phase . . .

The Second Step on the Mourning Trail

With the passing of those first few days, the shock and the numbness go, too, leaving the pain and agony in full force and all the terrible emotions breaking over the head of the mourner. We've covered this too often to repeat it again, except that this is the worst of the grief, the acute stage which stretches over the first six months or so. The healing, too, starts here, and things do ease after the first few weeks, say two to four—after this the mourner is on the road back and the difference is apparent. However, during this time, one must be on guard against oneself—the mourner can't fully trust himself or herself, or memory or emotions or reactions. The anger and guilt and other affects are barely under the mourner's control—anger and guilt and tearing sorrow can explode unexpectedly at any time, for this is the most booby-trapped part of the road back and almost anything can set off one of the mines. Open a drawer or a thought, stumble on a memento, see something in a shop window, pass an anniversary or holiday—almost anything can set off the raw anguish of the loss and the grief.

The pain of the grief must be accepted, for the work of grief, the healing of a wound, is a slow, painful process. But healing must go on if the mourner is to be whole again and if he or she is to achieve the growth and gain that are possible. Healing can only take place in a clean wound, and the grief wound can only be cleansed by the mourner, by looking deeply into his or her own feelings.

Anger with the deceased is one of the hardest things to deal with but must be faced up to despite the guilt it arouses. We're all ambivalent about those we love, but when death intervenes before anger is worked out there is guilt, and this makes grief work painful. It's never easy to face up to one's whole life, but grief forces one into it, to think through one's whole life in a short time. All the things we've already discussed come into play and take their toll as well. But there is vast change—new relationships inside as well as outside must now be established—and this is never easy. If one is fortunate enough to have had parents who showed the way to growth and change through separation and loss, then the way is easier but it is always difficult—just a matter of degree.

Each mourner must face up to his or her own special brand of hurt and think it through until gradually the storm subsides—the anger (with the world, with the deceased, with fate, with oneself) begins to disappear as does the guilt, the sadness eases, the emptiness and loss are less painful. But it all comes only through a reëxamination of all one's life, of one's values and philosophy. Here is where the awareness of the finite nature of our lives, the meaning of all life and new growth, make it possible to get the most out of life. Here, then, is the growth with grief, but it comes slowly and with much pain.

This is a time when the knowing person must recognize his or her own limited rationality, his or her still-confused thinking and feeling. Decisions of major importance to one's life should still be put off (we will discuss this shortly). But the first six months end with the mourner well along the road back, in better command of himself or herself and his or her emotions, with the storm definitely on the wane, although still likely to strike up afresh without warning. And so the mourner finds himself or herself on . . .

The Third Stage of the Mourning Trail

Recovery is now well on its way and moves with increasing speed and power as the second six months wind their way. The bereaved are now well able to shoulder their normal responsibilities, to see things more clearly, to be more comfortable with themselves and with the world about them. Finally the mourner is looking about him or her as he or she moves down the road back. Interest in the world about begins to return. The patterns of the first six months are present to a lesser and lesser degree. Sadness and sorrow and pain are giving way to nostalgia, and pleasant memories begin to intrude on the other remembrances. The difficulties begin to fade.

If the mourning patterns of the second stage are *not* reducing, it might well be wise to seek professional consultation. Something may have interfered with the healing process, and professional care and help may be needed to permit a return to health.

True, this recovery will end with a crash—the first anniversary of the death—but this, too, is normal; it won't happen this way again. Even the marked difference between the violence of this reaction and of those three months, six months, ten months before will be obvious, and so the mourner enters the last lap.

The Rest of the Road: Restitution and Recovery

The second year should pretty much see energy levels back to pre-grief levels, but the grieving itself may go on, as recent research indicates, for two or three years, particularly when a spouse is lost. There are some indications that mourning may be indefinite for a husband, certainly is permanent for a child. However, there should be a return to full functioning in the second year, and a failure to do so means professional help is needed. Reactions—sadness, feelings of loneliness and nostalgia, some pain—are bound to occur at certain times (the anniversaries or other meaningful times), but these should be passing experiences and increasingly fleeting as the years pass.

There are, however, certain things that are important to know about the road back, pitfalls and especially dangerous booby traps, which we will now cover in detail for the mourner.

Doctors, Surgery and Pills

Bereavement carries with it a high risk of illness so it is wise for the mourner to have a thorough medical checkup by the family doctor. Immediately after the loss might not be a bad time, since it may be helpful for the mourner to have some medication for a few days or even on occasion for sleep. But to protect oneself from the tendency of the medical profession in general to push pills, it would be best to ask, "Is there any point, Doctor, to my taking any medication, or will it be best to just suffer along until I find some peace on my own?"

If the mourner has the right kind of family physician, he or she will make time to talk out some of the grief problems. With the right kind of doctor, a number of visits to talk things out might be worthwhile and help ease the process. Should there be physical difficulties—a severe "allergic" skin reaction in one man I asked, intestinal cramps in another—it is best at this time to ask, "Doctor, is this simply an emotional reaction to my loss [should he push an Rx at the mourner]? Should I take anything, or would it be better to see a specialist, a psychiatrist or psychologist, to get at the roots of the problem?"

The physician who pooh-poohs this type of help or shoves pills at mourners for round-the-clock taking is not the one to use. But any physician is likely to give them to you if you approach him with, "Doc, can I have a tranquilizer like Mrs. So-and-So's physician gave *her?*" Regularly used mood-altering drugs and particularly those given during the daytime can hinder mourning and even prevent the necessary grief work, thus preventing healing. Mourners should never take mood drugs given by friends or relatives, no matter how well-meaning.

Unfortunately, Americans tend to forget that alcohol itself is a drug, and the worst offender so far as addiction is concerned. All those who have studied bereavement seem to feel that alcohol is the worst offender here, perhaps because people don't take it as seriously as they should and perhaps in part because it's so easy to get and everybody else is taking it. The same person who might hesitate to buy an over-the-counter tranquilizer or be careful with pills doctors give him or her won't hesitate to take that extra drink even though alcoholism is a serious danger.

Optional surgery is another area that should be avoided during bereavement, when the procedure is a matter of choice, say a hernia operation or varicose vein surgery which can be done a year or two later without harm or is just for cosmetic reasons. For one thing, the mourner's judgment isn't that good, and for another, surgery itself is a loss, and the bereaved has enough to cope with without adding additional fuel to the fire. Even more common though is . . .

Moving, Vacations and Sex

These may seem strange things to put together, but actually they do tend to fall into the same group on a psychological basis. There are people who cope with their emotional problems by involvement in external actions of many kinds. Rather than suffer through and resolve the painful emotional turmoil of bereavement, they try to run away from it by traveling (the "trip around the world" of the wealthy mourner, the "vacation" of the less well fixed, supposedly to forget and relax).

But, just as you can't leave your own shadow behind, so you can't escape from the problems of grief without going through the work of mourning. If these feelings are repressed or denied, they will only show themselves in a whole host of ways—physically (the psychosomatic disorders such as hypertension, intestinal problems, skin conditions and the like) and emotionally (anxieties, phobias, terrible feelings of impending doom, starting fights and so on).

This type of person may well decide to sell his or her home and move suddenly. Real-estate agents tell of the enormous numbers of widows who come to them immediately after their husbands' deaths, intent on selling their houses. Yet a year later these same widows are right back again with the agent—now seeking to repurchase the very house they sold. Similarly, many bereaved will suddenly turn promiscuous in a futile attempt to deal with the emptiness and loneliness and sadness of grief by going to bed in a whole succession of different arms. Like all attempts to solve emotional problems by physical actions, all these fail.

It's always wise to remember that to travel the road back takes slow, foot-slogging work—there's no quick shortcut. It takes time and pain to heal the wounds of bereavement, and grief work. Of all these actions, only a trip or vacation can help, if not taken for the wrong reasons or in the wrong way but thought out.

To dash off to a resort where one is unknown in new and unfamiliar surroundings with people who are mostly or all paired and are having lots of fun is likely to make the mourner feel even more isolated and alone and miserable than being at home among caring friends and familiar surroundings even though they do carry painful memories. The memories will go with the mourner, particularly in the beginning. But a wisely chosen short trip with someone close, to a place the mourner knows and likes, perhaps where the mourner will be occupied with things not intimately connected with the deceased can help. But the problems do go on.

Dealing with the Possessions of the Deceased

This is one of the most painful tasks the bereaved face. There are the clothes which many mourners prefer to give to close friends or relatives of the deceased. A number of widows have told me they had a good feeling even years later to see a close friend or brother of their husband wearing a favorite item of the deceased's clothing.

But the danger here, too, is of oversudden actions: throwing out books, paintings, favorite pieces of furniture or personal possessions (pens, watches and the like). After the pain has died down the survivor often finds a good deal of pleasure in, say, wearing a husband's or father's watch. As nostalgia takes over from sheer painful memories, many things become important for their associations, which may have a tinge of sadness, perhaps, but a good deal of pleasure in them once more. Apart from the clothing which can't be used by the survivor, other decisions on joint or personal possessions are best postponed until they can be approached with some perspective, say a year or two after the death. One friend of mine has only now gone through her husband's desk, three years after his death. It would have been too painful before, and she couldn't have judged what she found with any degree of wisdom.

Here as with moving or major decisions of any kind, the chief thing to remember is to take one's time—it takes years to recover from grief, and decisions should be put off for at least a year wherever possible. But one thing is clear. . .

The Wonder of Work

Keeping busy is almost uniformly helpful to widows—whether with business or housework or just doing or making things—as long as it can distract and take up time and energy while still being within the bereaved's capacity. The very fact that a confused, unsure, disorganized mourner can do something useful and do it properly offers proof and reassurance that this grief state is not a permanently damaging condition.

Going to work—often for the first time—has a special value for widows: it assures them that they are useful, promises financial help at a time when it is usually badly needed, and helps to bring them into social contact with adults, for, now without husbands, they might be limited to a world of children were they to stay home caring for their offspring. For all mourners, going to work means moving back into a normal social network which is of itself reassuring and helps the mourner to forget his or her loss. Work is always helpful, too, because it is often creative and by its very nature always productive.

Social and Sexual Participation

Whether it's a matter of a social life—visiting, parties, meetings or dating—this must be restored to normal sooner or later. But just when a mourner moves back into this and how is something the person must feel comfortable with—it happens almost by itself, and it is self-limiting. The bereaved do it by themselves, when they finally feel up to it. A failure to do so is another indication that professional help is needed. This process should also be well under way by the end of the first year and usually much earlier with ordinary social contacts. Dating—like sex—must set its own pace and happen when it feels right to the individual, but there is no real timetable here.

Which brings us now to . . .

The End of Mourning: Breaking with the Past

In today's Western societies there is usually no longer the ritualistic or religious end of mourning; there is in fact little to signal this time, so the individual has to find his or her own way out of the state. Perhaps reaching a point of freedom from the past signals the end to the individual without needing an official termination. Today, mourners must in most cases bring their own mourning "to an end as a tale that is told" as the Psalms put it.

Breaking with the past, accepting the deceased as dead, cutting the final ties so that the mourner is once more free to make his or her emotional investment in another person are needed. For the widow or widower, this may be signaled by sexual or emotional involvement with another person, perhaps even remarriage or the serious consideration in terms of a certain person. Thus, unlike Queen Victoria, each person must bring his or her mourning to its own end in his or her own way. When this does not happen, when the mourning does not end, then professional help is clearly needed. But for those who seek only support and a mutual sharing of problems, there are organizations available.

Support and Comfort: The Organizations That Help

There are today organizations available in a number of countries that offer help to the bereaved, some specifically to widows and widowers. Their area of interest varies and unfortunately only a limited number are national in scope. Here are some of those most widespread in English-speaking countries, along with some suggestions on how to seek local ones in one's own community, along with suggestions on starting one's own.

UNITED STATES

Parents Without Partners is both national and international, nonsectarian and nonprofit. Started in 1956 at New York's Jones Beach, the first meeting had twenty-five single parents, until today the organization spreads across the United States with some five hundred chapters here as well as in Canada and Australia and a membership of over sixty thousand single-parent families. The title tells who is eligible for membership and the local telephone book tells the address and phone number, at least in the sizable communities.

Theos (*T*hey *H*elp *E*ach *O*ther *S*piritually) is another national organization with chapters in Pittsburgh and Chambersburg, Pennsylvania, Salem, Oregon, and Seattle, Washington, but more are likely to be organized throughout the United States. This is to help young and middle-aged widowed persons rebuild their lives and cope with their problems of bereavement. It has no by-laws, constitution or dues and its home base is in Pittsburgh.

Naim is primarily in and around Chicago, and was originally

Catholic, but some non-Catholics have founded groups in their own churches. It is for the widowed person.

Post Cana is an association of widowed persons in the metropolitan area of Washington, D.C. Part of the Family Life Movement sponsored by the Archdiocese of Washington, it is open to the widowed of all denominations, although the priest of each area provides guidance.

Actually there are a large number of organizations, particularly for the widowed, scattered in communities large and small across the United States. Most seem to be affiliated with local churches, particularly the Catholic, but there are other programs such as the Widow-to-Widow and hot line set up by the Laboratory of Community Psychiatry of Harvard Medical School, or the Widows Consultation Center in New York City. The best local source of information would seem to be the ministers rather than the physicians, although both may know what is available. Local social service agencies commonly have this information also. Addresses have been omitted here simply because these do change and are often more confusing and misleading than helpful. The information above, however, will indicate where these organizations can be located in the telephone books.

GREAT BRITAIN

Self-help groups in England are more widespread and active than in the United States.

Cruse is a national organization for widows and their children. Its headquarters are in Richmond, Surrey.

The Society of Compassionate Friends in Coventry, Warwickshire, is chiefly for parents who have lost a child or expect to do so shortly.

For those who would want to set up their own local programs, an excellent way to start can be found in a book, *Helping Each*

Other in Widowhood, edited by Phyllis Silverman who founded the Widow-to-Widow program at Harvard. The book has a number of the local programs in various communities listed as well as information on the Harvard program and how it was started and operated.

But for the mourner there really should be repeated a warning —beware of that first year! It is a difficult year, and mostly because the thinking is so confused and the person just doesn't realize it by himself or herself at the time. It is not the time to make any major decisions or take any definitive actions that can possibly be put off safely until after the first anniversary of the death of the loved one.

Grief and mourning are natural processes, and they heal by themselves in most of us. It may seem hard to believe when one is going through it all, but one can only repeat Abe Lincoln's story in connection with mourning. It seems a Persian monarch ordered his wise men to prepare a short saying he could inscribe inside his ring to stand him in good stead both in good times and in bad.

After a year they brought the ring back and inside was engraved: AND THIS TOO SHALL PASS!

And with grief it does, but in its passing one can grow with the grief, find gain in the loss—this is the challenge and the promise of all grief and mourning.

Bibliography

Ariès P. *Western Attitudes toward Death*. Baltimore: Johns Hopkins University Press, 1974.

Becker, E. *The Denial of Death*. New York: The Free Press, 1973.

Bermann, E. *Scapegoat*. Ann Arbor: University of Michigan Press, 1973.

Bruehl, R.G. "Mourning, Family Dynamics and Pastoral Care," in *Death And Ministry* by J.D. Bane, et al. New York: Seabury Press, 1975.

Campbell, J. *The Hero with a Thousand Faces*. Cleveland: World Publishing, 1964.

Castelnuovo-Tedesco, P. Personal communications.

———— *Psychiatric Aspects of Organ Transplantation*. New York: Grune & Stratton, 1971.

Clayton, P.J., et al. "The Bereavement of the Widowed." *DIS. NERV. SYS.*, 32: 597, 1971.

———— "Mortality and Morbidity in The First Year of Widowhood." *ARCH. GEN. PSYCH.*, 30: 747, 1974.

———— "A Study of Normal Bereavement." *AMER. J. PSYCHIAT.*, 125: 64, 1968.

Cutter, F. *Coming to Terms With Death*. Chicago: Nelson-Hall, 1974.

Danto, B.L. "Drug Ingestion and Suicide During Anticipatory Grief," in *Anticipatory Grief* by B. Schoenberg, et al. New York: Columbia University Press, 1974.

Davidson, G.W. "Waiting Vulture Syndrome," in *Bereavement* by B. Schoenberg, et al. New York: Columbia University Press, 1975.

Degnan, M., et al. "Genetic Counseling." *Amer. Fam. Physician*, 12: 110, 1975.

Engel, G.L. "Signs of Giving Up," in *The Patient, Death, and the Family* by Troup and Greene. New York: Charles Scribner's Sons, 1974.

Freud, S. *Mourning and Melancholia*. 1915.

Furman, E. *A Child's Parent Dies*. New Haven: Yale University Press, 1974.

Furman, R.A. "The Child's Reaction to Death in the Family," in *Loss And Grief* by B. Schoenberg, et al. New York: Columbia University Press, 1970.

Glick, I.O., et al. *The First Year of Bereavement*. New York: John Wiley, 1974.

Gorer, G. *Death, Grief and Mourning*. London: Cresset Press, 1965.

Grollman, E.A. *Explaining Death to Children*. Boston: Beacon Press, 1969.

Gunderson, E.K.E., and Rahe, R.H. *Life, Stress and Illness*. Springfield: Charles C. Thomas, 1974.

Hilgard, J.R. "Depressive and Psychotic States as Anniversaries." *Int. Psychiatry Clinics*, VI:197, 1969.

Hinton, J. *Dying*, 2nd Ed. Middlesex, England: Penguin Books, 1972.

Holmes, T.H., and Masuda, M. "Life Change and Illness Susceptibility," in *Stressful Life Events* by Dohrenwend and Dohrenwend. New York: John Wiley, 1974.

Kavanaugh, R.E. *Facing Death*. Los Angeles: Nash Publishing, 1972.

Kliman, G. *Psychological Emergencies of Childhood*. New York: Grune & Stratton, 1971.

Krant, M.J. *Dying and Dignity*. Springfield: Charles C. Thomas, 1974.

Kubler-Ross, E. *Death the Final Stage of Growth*. Englewood Cliffs: Prentice-Hall, 1975.

———— *On Death and Dying*. New York: MacMillan, 1969.

Maddison, D. et al. "The Health of Widows in the Year Following Bereavement." *J. Psychosom. Research*, 12:297, 1968.

———— "Conjugal Bereavement and the Social Network," in *Bereavement* by Schoenberg, et al. New York: Columbia University Press, 1972.

Marris, P. *Loss and Change*. New York: Pantheon Books, 1974.

Mitchell, E.M. *The Child's Attitude to Death*. New York: Schocken, 1967.

Parkes, C.M. *Bereavement*. New York: Intl. University Press, 1972.

———— "The First Year of Bereavement." *Psychiatry*, 33: 444, 1970.

———— "Broken Heart." *British Med. J.*, 1: 740, 1969.

Pincus, L. *Death and the Family*. New York: Pantheon Books, 1974.

Pollock, G.H. Personal communication.

———— "Temporal Anniversary Manifestations." *PSA. Quarterly*, XL:123, 1971.

———— "Mourning and Adaptation." *INT. J. PSA.*, XLII:341, 1961.

Rees, W.D. "The Hallucinations of Widowhood." *Brit. Med. J.*, 2 Oct. 1971: 37.

————, et al. "Mortality of Bereavement." *Brit. Med. J.*, 7 Oct. 1967: 13.

Rosenblatt, P.C. "Uses of Ethnography in Understanding Grief and Mourning," in *Bereavement* by Schoenberg, et al. New York: Columbia University Press, 1975.

Schoenberg, B., et al. *Bereavement*. New York: Columbia University Press, 1975.

Schowalter, J.E. "Parent Death and Child Bereavement," in *Bereavement* by Schoenberg, et al. New York: Columbia University Press, 1975.

Schwab, J.J., et al. "Studies in Grief," in *Bereavement* by Schoenberg, et al. New York: Columbia University Press, 1975.

Sheatsley, P.B., and Feldman, J.J. "The Assassination of President Kennedy." *Pub. Opinion Quat.*, XXVIII:189, 1964.

Silverman, P. *Helping Each Other in Widowhood*. New York: Health Sciences Publishing, 1974.

Solecki, R.S. "Neanderthal is Not An Epithet." *Sci. Amer.*, May 1971: 20.

Toch, R. "Bereavement: A Pediatric View," in *Death and Ministry* by J.D. Bane. New York: Seabury Press, 1975.

Vernon, G.M. *Sociology of Death*. New York: Ronald Press, 1970.

Volkan, V.D. Personal communications.

―――― "The Recognition and Prevention of Pathological Grief." *Va. Med. Monthly*, 99:535, 1972.

―――― "Normal and Pathological Grief Reactions." *Va. Med. Monthly*, 93:651, 1966.

―――― "The Linking Objects of Pathological Mourners." *Arch. Gen. Psychiat.* 27:215, 1972.

Wessel, M.A. "Adolescents and the Death of a Parent," in *Medical Care of the Adolescent*, 3rd Ed. by J.R. Gallagher et al. New York: Appleton, Century Crofts, 1976: Chap. 26 (p. 264).

White, R.B., and Gathman, L.I. "The Syndrome of Ordinary Grief." *Amer. Family Physician*, 8:96, 1973.

Young, M., et al. "The Mortality of Widowers." *Lancet*, 2:454, 31 Aug. 1963.

Index